Samuel Sharp, John Rivington

Letters from Italy

describing the customs and manners of that country, in the years 1765, and 1766.

Third Edition

Samuel Sharp, John Rivington

Letters from Italy

describing the customs and manners of that country, in the years 1765, and 1766. Third Edition

ISBN/EAN: 9783337088989

Printed in Europe, USA, Canada, Australia, Japan

Cover: Foto ©ninafisch / pixelio.de

More available books at **www.hansebooks.com**

LETTERS

FROM

ITALY,

DESCRIBING THE

CUSTOMS and MANNERS
of that COUNTRY,

In the YEARS 1765, and 1766.

To which is ANNEXED,

An ADMONITION to GENTLEMEN who pass the ALPS, in their Tour through ITALY.

By SAMUEL SHARP, Esq.

The THIRD EDITION.

LONDON:
Printed for HENRY and CAVE at St John's-Gate; and sold by J. RIVINGTON; R. BALDWIN; S. CROWDER; T. LONGMAN; HAWES CLARKE and COLLINS; J. JOHNSON and Co; T. Caslon; W. NICOL; S. BLADON; and F. NEWBERRY.

PREFACE.

THE Reader will plainly perceive that the following LETTERS, though now a little altered and curtailed, were not originally intended for the Prefs. My Correspondents, who preserved them, have persuaded me to believe they may possibly amuse the World; but, had I foreseen this Publication, I might, with very little Trouble, have been circumstantial in many Particulars where I am now superficial.

Before I left *England*, I was fully apprised of the Danger a Traveller is exposed to, of mistaking Singularities for Customs, and hope I have guarded against that Error. I had known several *Frenchmen*, who, having acquired *English* enough to read a News Paper, believed that Treaties of Marriage in *England* are usually negociated by Advertisements. I was once acquainted with a poor starving Gentleman at *Paris*, who knew no more of the History of *England* than the Fate of our unhappy Kings, *Charles* I. and *James* II. I have heard this poor Man, with Tears in his Eyes, thank the *bon Dieu* that he was not born a King of *England*. At this present Time, I know a very sensible and learned *Italian*, who being curious to examine the Truth of a popular

pular Opinion in *Italy*, *That no Englishman fears Death*, prevailed upon himself to attend the Execution of my Lord *Lovat*, and Mr *Radcliffe*. It is very well remembered with what singular Tranquillity and Heroism those Gentlemen died; but this Accident has confirmed, as he imagines, the Truth of that Opinion. Instructed by such Lessons, I flatter myself that I have not often been too hasty in judging of the Customs and Manners of *Italy*.

Should the more reasonable Catholicks of *England* think I have been too particular in my Descriptions of the superstitious Practices of their Religion, I must beg Leave to remind them of their own frequent Declarations, that, in this enlightened Age, those Pageantries are continued abroad, merely to comply with the Weakness of the ignorant Multitude, who would imagine the Fundamentals of their Faith shaken by any Retrenchment of those Ceremonies; and, if this be their Avowal, certainly what a Papist disapproves of, a Protestant may describe without giving Offence.

LETTER

LETTER I.

VENICE, *September* 1765.

DEAR SIR,

WE are arrived at *Venice* by the road of *Geneva, Turin, Milan, Verona, Vicenza* and *Padua*; but as my residence in these cities has not been of sufficient continuance to give me more than a superficial idea of all that I have seen or heard, I shall not communicate what observations I have made, till my return; when, perhaps, a second visit, and a farther acquaintance with the manners of *Italy*, will enable me to judge better of men and things. I do not mean to trouble you, or my other Friends, during my stay abroad, with descriptions of statues, churches, and pictures; for, besides, that I can say no more on that subject than what every account of *Italy*, every guide for travellers, furnishes in a most tedious abundance, I have generally found the reading of such descriptions insipid and tiresome; indeed, how can it be otherwise, since the touches of a *Raphael*, or *Michael Angelo*, must be seen to be admired, and are no more susceptible of a description in words, than is the air of a musical composition. These accounts, however, are both pleasant and useful in the hands of a traveller, who, if he compare them with the originals, will borrow a thousand hints, which would otherwise escape the most diligent observer.

I must confess to you that I have yet seen nothing which has afforded me so much pleasure as that extraordinary Genius Monsf. *Voltaire*. My principal motive for passing the *Alps*, by the way of *Geneva*, was a visit to that Gentleman. I knew him in the days of my youth, and had the honour to be sometimes with him when he was in *London*. I also saw him at *Paris* in 1749, and now that he is become the topic of conversation in almost every village in *Europe*, I could not think of going to *Italy* without granting myself the indulgence of seeing him once more. He lives about four miles from *Geneva*, in a most splendid and hospitable manner, keeping an open table, to which strangers of every nation

tion, find an easy introduction. Contiguous to his house is a small theatre, which holds about fifty people, but, when enlarged, will contain two hundred; the carpenters were beginning the alteration the day I dined with him. Perhaps he never had been more happy in any one period of his life than at the juncture I saw him. Mademoiselle *Clairon*, who has quitted the stage, was on a visit there, and had exhibited that week in two characters of his own writing. I unfortunately arrived at *Geneva* the night after she had performed for the last time. I had often seen her in 1749; but I found by *Voltaire*, that, excellent as she was in those days, she had improved in the last sixteen years beyond all imagination. I cannot give you an idea of the ecstacies he was in, acting and repeating, every now and then, a hundred passages, where she had been particularly happy in her expression. His eyes have such a brilliancy in those moments, that you forget he is above seventy-two. He had that morning written an epistle to Mad. *Clairon*, in verse, which he read to the company from the foul copy: There were some erasements in it, but not many. To perform a play, he is obliged to seize the opportunity, when any ftroling comedians come into the neighbourhood of *Geneva*; with some of these, and a niece who lives with him, he then entertains himself and friends; but the visit of Madam *Clairon* had given a perfection to this last spectacle which he had never hoped for.

I wish, for the honour of my country, it were possible that a *Frenchman* could taste the language of *Shakespeare*: I am persuaded, could *Voltaire* feel the energy of our Poet's descriptions, he would talk no more of his Barbarisms, and his *some beauties*. He who has so great a share of merit himself, would gladly pay the tribute due to the shrine of *Shakespeare*, and, possibly, grieve to have attempted those translations which he has presented to his countrymen as a specimen of *Shakespeare*'s manner of writing. It is true, he apologises for the faintness of the execution; but still, had he felt the excessive inferiority of his imitations; had he known so well as *Englishmen* do, that they have not the least resemblance of the strength, spirit, and imagination of the original, he certainly would never have hazarded the publication. I remember to have heard him say, about the

year

year 1726, that, before he learnt *English*, he had read the *Spectators* in *French*, and often wondered that such dull writings should please a polite nation; "But now," said he, "that I have acquired the tongue, I wipe my b——h with *Plutarch!*" The phrase was too remarkable, and made too strong an impression on the ears of a young man, to be ever forgotten.

This story I would apply to *Voltaire* himself, and to every *Frenchman* who learns *English* after he is twenty-five years of age. Tho' they may be sufficiently instructed to relish the good sense, and, possibly, the wit and humour of our *Spectators* in prose, the powers of *Shakespeare* in measure, will always remain unfelt. They may understand the construction, as a school-boy reads *Virgil*; but they never will catch the fire. If *Voltaire* found so much difference betwixt the original and translation of the *Spectators*, I do not doubt, but with a thorough knowledge of *English*, he would find as much, or more, betwixt the *Shakespeare* he now reads, and the *Shakespeare* he would then feel.

I am, Sir, &c.

LETTER II.

VENICE, *Sept.* 1765.

SIR,

WE came from *Padua* to *Venice*, by the river *Brenta*, in a private boat. There are boats which set out every day, to and from *Padua*, like our stage-coaches, and carry passengers for about a shilling; but it is usual for people of a certain rank, to take a vessel to themselves. It is larger than a *Gravesend* boat, and is provided with a room built in the middle, and covered in, big enough to hold twenty persons at least; every expence included, it costs an *English* company about thirty-five shillings. The river *Brenta* is famous for the beauty of the country houses built on its banks, which here, as through all *Italy*, bear the name of palaces. We did not disembark, to visit the gardens of these palaces, and, therefore, cannot give our judgment upon the subject; but they are much celebrated by the people of the country. When you arrive within four or five miles of *Venice*, at a place called *Fusina*, where the river opens into the *Laguna*,

(lake)

LETTER II.

(lake) on which the city and adjacent iflands are fituated, you hire gondolas. Here a wonderful fcene opens to every ftranger, when he firft cafts his eye on this enchanting profpect. There are few Gentlemen who are not, in fome degree, apprized of what they are to expect from the views they have feen of this place, painted by *Canaletti*; neverthelefs, the real object exceeds, in beauty, what the imagination is led to conceive from thefe draughts; which, however, feldom happens, as the reprefentation of buildings in pictures is generally more gaudy and flattering than the life itfelf. Here the fuel, being wood, there is no dirty fmoak to deface the heavens, the water, and the buildings. There are no dirty barges, nor dirty men; for the Barcaroles (Gondaliers) have moft of them an elegant waterman's livery, and the others, who are not in Gentlemens fervice, being a fober body of men, are not in rags, like the lower fort of people in *England*, who fpend all they can get in porter, or fpirituous liquors.

In *Venice* there is one large canal, which runs through the middle of the city, in this form,

form ⌒ and which receives into it a prodigious number of smaller canals. Almost every house has one door communicating with a street, and another opening immediately upon a canal. There are a few canals from which you land into a narrow street, betwixt the house and the canal. The houses, the gondolas, and the canals, were there no other curiosity, would be very amusing; but the delights of this place are the views of the islands in the neighbourhood. South of the city is another range of buildings and canals, called *Giudecca*; they are divided by a canal, of the breadth of the *Thames* at *London*; and here an airing upon the water, is the diversion of the *Sunday* evening, and festivals, an hour before dark. The ladies, with their *Cavalieri Servanti*, (called *Cicisbei* in other parts of *Italy*) row backwards and forwards near the bank of the *Giudecca*, as, in former days, our gentry in *England* frequented the ring in *Hyde-Park*.

In the way to the *Lazaretto*, the island where quarantine is performed, you pass in sight of several islands, where the churches, convents, &c. furnish an abundant entertainment to the Virtuosi, who have a taste for *Palladio*, *Titian*, *Paul Veronese*, &c. One of the

LETTER II.

the most curious sights we saw amongst these curiosities, was the famous Mr ―— [*Wortley Montague*], who was performing quarantine at the *Lazaretto*. All the *English* made a point of paying him their compliments in that place, and he seemed not a little pleased with their attention. It may be supposed that visitors are not suffered to approach the person of any who is performing quarantine. They are divided by a passage of about seven or eight feet wide. Mr ―— [*Wortley Montague*] was just arrived from the East; he had travelled through the *Holy Land*, *Egypt*, *Armenia*, *&c.* with the Old and New Testament in his hands for his direction, which he told us had proved unerring guides. He had particularly taken the road of the *Israelites* through the wilderness, and had observed that part of the *Red Sea* which they passed through. He had visited *Mount Sinai*, and flattered himself he had been on the very part of the Rock where *Moses* spake face to face with God Almighty. His beard reached down to his breast, being of two years and a half growth; and the dress of his head was *Armenian*. He was in the most enthusiastic raptures with *Arabia*, and the *Arabs*; like theirs, his bed was the ground, his

food

food rice, his beverage water, his luxury a pipe and coffee. His purpose was to return once more amongst that virtuous people, whose morals and hospitality he said are such, that, were you to drop your cloak in the highway, you would find it there six months afterwards, an *Arab* being too honest a man to pick up what he knows belongs to another; and were you to offer money for the provision you meet with, he would ask you with concern, why you had so mean an opinion of his benevolence, to suppose him capable of accepting a gratification. Therefore money, said he, in that country, is of very little use, as it is only necessary for the purchase of garments, which, in so warm a climate, are very few, and of very little value. He distinguishes, however, betwixt the wild and the civilized *Arab*, and proposes to publish an account of all that I have written.

I should do an injustice to our resident, Mr *Murray*, did I not mention the politeness with which he receives us, and all his countrymen. I do not doubt, but that from a man of his understanding, and communicative disposition, I shall learn all a traveller would wish to know.

I am, Sir, &c.

LETTER III.

VENICE, *Sept.* 1765.

SIR,

VENICE, with a few alterations, would be much more magnificent than it now is: The windows, inftead of fafhes, are ftill as in the other parts of *Italy*, made of fmall panes of glafs, inclofed in lead, which is exceedingly paltry; and what is ftill worfe, they are covered with iron grates, exactly refembling thofe of our prifons, which makes a dreadful and gloomy view of the fronts of their palaces. Thefe grates were formerly called *Gelofias*, but I queftion whether they are now much known by that name; for never was fo entire a revolution effected in the manners of a nation, as in this inftance of jealoufy. In ancient days wives were immured in *Italy*, and hufbands were jealous: Now, no women on earth are under fo little reftraint, and the word jealoufy is become obfolete. The fhutters of their houfes are plain deal boards tacked together without the leaft form or decoration, and not painted like ours in *England*, fo that when a palace is fhut up, it

very

very much resembles a bridewell, or an hospital for lunaticks. They likewise lay on the roofs of their houses such heavy clumsy tiles, that they very much offend the eye. House-rent is remarkably cheap for so large and so trading a city. A house of seventy pounds a year I should have guessed at near two hundred, and so of others I enquired after.

The Republick is extremely rigid in what regards the quarantine; and, indeed, as they border upon those countries where the plague so frequently rages, they cannot be too watchful. There is not the least connivance ever practised; all letters, to whomsoever directed, are first opened by the officers, and then smoaked before they are delivered. Were Mr ———— to have handed over a news-paper to me, and we had been detected in the action, I must inevitably have performed quarantine in the *Lazaretto*, a certain number of weeks. A few years since, a boy got on board one of these vessels performing quarantine, and stole some tobacco; he was pursued into *Venice*, and shot dead in the streets. There are many custom-house officers in their boats, watching the quarantine night and day, who would certainly kill the first man

LETTER III.

man who should attempt to escape on shore, before the expiration of the quarantine.

Their churches, their pictures, and their arsenal, admit of no other observation than what is to be found in books upon that subject; I shall however mention one remark, that their men of war are built under cover, and not being exposed to the weather, are consequently less liable to decay.

The church called *Redemtore*, is a curious instance of the power of art; for though it is not to be ranked amongst the rich and expensive churches, abounding neither in gold nor marble, yet the simplicity and elegance of its structure had a wonderful influence on us the moment we entered within the door, and convinced us how deservedly *Palladio* is admired, and how possible it is to taste the beauty of proportion and design, without having studied the rudiments of the art.

I am, Sir, &c.

LETTER IV.

VENICE, *Sept.* 1765.

SIR,

I WAS present this morning in the Senate-house, at an election of some officers of the State. The *Venetian* Nobles have various methods of electing by ballot their magistrates and officers, according to the dignity of their office, but they resemble one another in the essential form so much, that the specimen I saw, will give you no bad idea of the whole. Supposing that there are several hundred Nobles present who are to vote, just so many hundred balls are put into a box, two hundred of which, or thereabout, are golden; those who take out the golden balls are entitled to vote, and for that purpose retire with the Doge and others into an adjacent room; so that, by this means, the candidates cannot know who are to be their electors. If, amongst those that have taken out the golden balls, there be any related to the candidates, they do not ballot, but stand neuter at one end of the room. The ballots of two hundred people are collected in half a minute, by about forty little boys from seven to eleven

ven years of age; they have each their several stations, where they collect the balls from a certain number of the Nobles; and running on their errand as fast as they can, a ballot for six or seven candidates is soon dispatched.

The theatres are not now open; but when they are, all the world goes thither, particularly in the season of the Carnival, where the Barcaroles (Gondaliers) make so great a figure, that it is said of them, what our *Bickerstaff* said of the trunk-maker in the *Tatler*, that what they censure or applaud, is generally condemned or approved by the publick: in short, that it is the Barcaroles who decide the fate of an Opera or Play. These Barcaroles are certainly such a body of sober men as in *England* we have no instance of amongst the lower class of people: In masking-time, however, they indulge the taste of gaming, and, doubtless, often play with the Nobles their masters; but the brownness and coarseness of their hands betray their occupation; besides that it is impossible for them to forbear making their boasts, or their complaints, of good and bad fortune, when their dialect and deportment never fail to discover them.

The number as well as the character of this people renders their body very respectable: When one considers, that in all the great families, every Gentleman keeps a distinct gondola, rowed by two men, except some few who have but one rower, it will be readily conceived that the number of Barcaroles must be very considerable. They are exceedingly proud of their station, and with some reason; for their profession leads them into the company of the greatest men of the state, and it is the fashion to converse with them, to hear their wit and humour, and applaud all they say; besides, the pay of a Barcarole is about eighteen pence a day, with liveries and little perquisites, which, in so cheap a country, is a plentiful income to a sober man: accordingly, it is notorious, that all of them can afford to marry, and do marry.

The manner of rowing a gondola, standing and looking forward, may be seen in every view of *Venice*, and this manner is absolutely necessary for the guidance of a boat in these narrow canals; but it is curious to observe how dexterous they are by use; for it is very rare that they touch, much less endanger over-setting, though they are every instant

LETTER IV.

instant within half an inch of each other. One cannot be an hour on these canals without seeing several of the Barcaroles shifting themselves; for it is a custom amongst them to have always a dry shirt ready to put on, the moment after they have landed their fare; and they would expect to die, if by any accident they were under the necessity of suffering a damp shirt to dry on their bodies. On the other hand, it is curious to observe how careless they are of damp sheets through all *Italy*, and the people at inns are so little apprised of an objection to damp sheets, that when you begin to beg they would hang them before the fire, they desire you will feel how wet they are, being prepossessed that you mean they have not been washed: In fact, unless you have servants who will dry them for you, it is in vain to expect it should be done.

By a sumptuary law of the State, all the gondolas must be black, so that their appearance is very dismal; and every body, at first sight, compares the cabin you sit in, to a hearse. The nobles too, by a sumptuary law, cannot wear a sword, and are obliged to dress in black, and long wigs. *I am, Sir, &c.*

LETTER. V.

Venice, *Sept.* 1765.

SIR,

GALLANTRY is so epidemical in this city, that few of the Ladies escape the contagion. No woman can go into a public place, but in the company of a Gentleman, called here, a *Cavaliére Servente*, and in other parts of *Italy*, a *Cicesbeo*. This Cavaliere is always the same person; and she not only is attached to him, but to him singly; for frequently no other woman joins the company, but it is usual for them to sit alone in the box at the opera or play-house, where they must be, in a manner, by themselves, as the theatres are so very dark that the spectators can hardly be said to be in company with one another. After the Opera, the Lady, and her *Cavaliére Servente* retire to her Casine, where they have a *Tete-a-Tete* for an hour or two, and then her visitors join them for the rest of the evening, or night; for on some festival and jolly days, they spend the whole night, and take Mass in their way home. You must

know

know a Cafine is nothing more than a fmall room, generally at or near St *Mark's Place*, hired for the moſt part by the year, and facred to the Lady and her Cavaliére; for the huſband never approaches it. On the other hand, the huſband has his revenge; for he never fails to be the *Cavaliere Servente* of fome other woman; and, I am told, it would be fo ridiculous for a huſband to appear in public with his wife, that there is no inſtance of ſuch a phænomenon; and, therefore, it is impoſſible for a woman to bear up againſt the torrent of this faſhion. Were a young wife to flatter herſelf that ſhe had married a man for the love and eſteem ſhe bore to him, and that it would be injurious to his honour to paſs ſo many private hours with a *Cavaliere Servente*, what would be the conſequence? She muſt live for ever at home; no woman would dare to appear with her, and it would be impoſſible to find a man who would not exact the privileges of a *Cavaliere Servente*: Accordingly, it ſeldom happens that a bride holds out beyond a few months after marriage againſt this mode, and there are many examples where the Cavaliere, and not the huſband, is the object; where the Cavaliere is taken immediately into
ſervice,

service, and for whose sake the marriage is a pretext and screen.

So many opportunities must, therefore, render this Republick a second *Cyprus*, where all are votaries to *Venus*, unless it please Heaven to pour down more grace amongst them than falls to the share of other nations in this degenerate age; but the calumniators deny that the husbands believe in this partial favour, and assert, that they have very little fondness for their children, compared with the parents of other kingdoms: They are the children of the Republick, they say, but not so certainly the children of their reputed fathers: The girls, therefore, are early sent to convents, where they remain till they marry, or die, and are visited by their fathers and mothers seldom or never: if they marry, they at once burst out from a secluded life, and a narrow education, into the scene of licentiousness I have just described.

Some of these Cavalieri, according to the nature of the parties, are said to be very abject and servile, doing the meanest offices, and submitting to the grossest tyranny: Others have an ascendant over their mistresses, and there is often as much jealousy betwixt the Ladies

Ladies here, on the subject of their Cavalieri, as in other countries on account of their husbands; and it happens now and then, that the Ladies and Cavalieri separate in favour of others; but this seems to be a delicate point, and to be avoided as much as divorces are with us. The ambition, the rage for a Casine, is become so essential to fashionableness, that it is ludicrous to see how low it descends amongst people who wish to be esteemed the *beau-monde*. It is impossible to refrain from laughter when such or such a man is pointed out as going to his Casine; men that you know to have the gravest characters in every other place but a Casine, and whom you would rather have suspected of hypocrisy, superstition, and fanaticism, than of an avowed and publick gallantry.

This is the picture of *Venetian* amours in the present age; but Charity would lead one to hope the colours are laid on too strongly: Politicians, however, pretend to give an easy solution of this licentiousness amongst the Ladies: They tell you, that, in former times, the courtezans were a useful class of citizens, whose arms were always open to the wealthy, whether they were young or old; that now
they

they have no such character among them, and the stews that are connived at, receive only the very dregs of the people. Every dissolute man of fortune is, therefore, in a manner, driven into the practice of either keeping a mistress, or becoming a *Cavaliere Servente:* The former method is more expensive, and less honourable; the latter, consequently, the more prevalent.

The Bank of *Venice*, called here, the Bank of the *Rialto*, is a very small office, and the whole business is transacted by a few clerks, who sit in a small room, like an open booth, which faces the Exchange. The business of the Bank may be aptly compared to that of a Banker in *England*, where merchants deposit a large sum of money, and draw upon the shop for their disbursements. At *Venice*, every bill of exchange of above a hundred silver ducats, that is, so many times three shillings and four-pence, must be paid at the Bank. This method, in so large and so commercial a city as *London*, would be very inconvenient, but here, is extremely useful, as a transfer is finished in half a minute, which saves the trouble of weighing and examining the coin; a precaution absolutely necessary in this country, where many of the sequins are light; besides that no chicanery can be practised in case you lose the receipts, the transfer being a sufficient testimony of the payment. It may be presumed too, that the Republic has some private views in this ordinance, besides the benefit of the merchants; for, should any sudden exigency of the State occur, they have a quantity of cash in their hands for immediate use.

I am, Sir, &c.

LETTER VI.

VENICE, *Sept.* 1765.

SIR,

WE have this day seen a wedding, at *La Madona Della Pesta*, of two of the greatest families in *Venice*: I say families; for all matches are rather alliances of families, than attachments of the parties married. These marriages are generally publick, and the relations are desirous to have as many assistants and witnesses at church, as they can collect:

collect: It is usual upon this occasion to send an invitation to foreigners. All the women who are admitted, have likewise a formal invitation; but no Gentleman is denied entrance. The Ladies who are the acquaintance of the parties, appear as gawdy as their sumptuary laws will suffer them; but these laws oblige them to wear black, so that their laced ruffles and head-dress, with their diamonds, are the chief ornament; and, to say the truth, though their diamonds be numerous, they appear to great disadvantage by being ill set in a large quantity of silver. The number of the well-dressed Ladies was only fifteen; the rest of the women in the church were of low rank. The bride alone was dressed in white, with a long train; the bridegroom, in the usual black dress of a *Venetian* Noble, not unlike one of our Counsellor's in *England* with a Judge's wig. She was led up to the Altar by a *Venetian* Noble, where she kneeled, with her husband on her right hand. They both continued on their knees till the ceremony was finished, which, with the Mass, lasted above half an hour. She was then handed out of the church by the same Noble, and, as is the custom, she curtsied and paid her complements,

LETTER VI.

ments, in her return, to all her's and her husband's friends. Upon this occasion there are Epithalamiums printed, and made presents of to certain spectators and acquaintance. I should suppose that the poems I received, were of a size to sell for eight or nine shillings in *England*. It must happen, now and then, that a rich *Venetian* has no son; in which case, a daughter may be a great fortune; but, in general, a young Lady with six or seven thousand pounds, is esteemed a good fortune; for the ambition of the noble families is to unite, as much as possible, their riches with their name. The ladies here, as also at *Turin*, and *Milan*, are generally very fair: The men are not so handsome, but, I think, remarkably tall. Look at any class amongst them which cannot be selected, the Nobles for example, and you will find very few short men amongst them.

I am, Sir, &c.

LETTER VII.

VENICE, *Sept.* 1765.

SIR,

VENICE, from its fystem of policy, opens the doors of her nobles to very few ftrangers. No country in the world adheres more rigidly to her antient laws and cuftoms than this Republick. Amongft others, there is one ordinance that not only prohibits the nobles themfelves from holding the leaft intercourfe with foreign minifters; but it is fo very fevere, that fhould even one of their fervants pafs the threfhold of an ambaffador, he would infallably be fent to prifon: The law therefore renders the life of a foreign minifter exceedingly dull and unfociable; befides that it ftops the channel through which young gentlemen on their travels would naturally find accefs to the beft company. I believe the origin of this law at *Venice*, had its rife from a frivolous narrow conceit of confounding and preventing plots againft the ftate; but, in a fumptuary view, it may be ufeful, as it fuppreffes that emulation in luxury,

ury which the visits betwixt their nobles and the foreign ministers would naturally produce.

The Nobles are said to be above fifteen hundred in number, and it will therefore be readily supposed, that far the greater part of them are poor, as all the sons are noble, and they have no means of adding to their patrimony, but by obtaining magistracies and offices in the government, which are not lucrative, compared with *English* employments: for, by an antient act of the senate, a noble must not be concerned in any article of commerce, though it is whispered, that many of them have clandestine partnerships. The sons too, being all nobles, they divide their estates more equally than in monarchical kingdoms; where the eldest son only, in order to support the honour of the family with the greater splendor, enjoys the title and estate. It is true, that, in *Venice*, the eldest has some benefit from his primogeniture; but, as I have intimated, that benefit is not very considerable. It is the ambition of every Noble to marry one daughter to a Noble; on which account he sends the others to convents, that he may be better enabled to

give

give her a fortune, and provide handsomely for his sons.

There are four convents in *Venice*, to which four hospitals are annexed, that give names to the convents. They are of a very singular institution in one article, being open to a certain number of poor young women, who are thoroughly instructed in both vocal and instrumental musick. They exhibit in their churches, on particular days of the week and some festivals, (to the public gratis,) and are much followed, as the performance is finer than one expects in any other place than a theatre. The terms upon which they accept their education, are, to remain in the convent until their talents shall induce some one to marry them. This happens very rarely, so that they generally sing on till their voices are lost, and their names are forgotten. The founders of this charity had, as it appears, too exalted an opinion of the power of musick; for, however beautiful the girls may be, they trust only to their melody, being intercepted from the sight of the audience, by a black gauze hung over the rails of the gallery in which they perform: It is transparent

rent enough to shew the figures of women, but not in the least their features and complexion.

I am, Sir, &c.

LETTER VIII.

VENICE, Sept. 1765.

SIR.

THE poor people live very well in the city of *Venice*, which, however, may, in a great measure, be ascribed to their ignorance of gin and brandy. They love gaming, and are, consequently, often needy; but the Government connives at it, and is rather pleased to have them so: As for those who by sickness, or other accidents, are reduced to poverty, there is an abundance of charitable foundations; however, the swarms of beggars are surprizingly great. The trade of begging, in all catholic countries, will necessarily prosper, so long as that species of charity, which is bestowed on beggars, continues to be inculcated by their preachers and confessors, as the most perfect of all moral duties.

I must take notice of some disadvantages this city labours under. The water here is such an invitation to gnats, that no stranger to this place will conceive the torments we suffered every day and night from these insects; and, it must be granted, that the canals, at low water, are often, in the summer, very offensive, perhaps unwholesome. The bread is indifferent, and the wine, as through all *Italy* to this city, very bad. Living in the midst of salt water, all the water they drink, except what is brought from the *Brenta*, is collected from the rain which falls on their houses: To this end they dig a well, which at a certain depth, they surround with a wall of terras, made very compact, that the salt water in the canals may not transude into the well: Then they lay a bed of sand, thro' which the rain water filters into the well, as they imagine, in the most perfect state of purity: However, as every housekeeper thinks his well better finished than that of his neighbour, one may conclude that some of them are porous, and do admit more or less salt-water into them. The frequency of diarrhœas in this city, is another argument, that the water they drink is purgative; but perhaps one of the greatest inconveniencies of these wells, is, that they do not contain water enough

nough for a family, in long droughts, which frequently happen in *Italy*.

All pleadings at the bar muſt be in the *Venetian* dialect, which is unpleaſant to the ear of a foreigner; and though none but an *Italian* ſhould dare to criticiſe on the ſtile and taſte of an *Italian*, yet a foreigner may venture to pronounce, that the *Venetian* dialect is a corrupt *Italian*, as they have letters in their alphabet, which moſt of the natives of this town can never learn to utter; and are therefore obliged to drop entirely, or to ſubſtitute others in their place. For example, in all words where the letter *g* is introduced, this obſervation takes place; for, inſtead of pronouncing it in the words *Giudice, Giulio, Giovanne*, and a thouſand others, they ſay *Dudice, Dulio, Diovanne*, &c. and in the words *Mangiare, Ragione*, they drop it almoſt entirely, and ſay *Maniare, Raione*, &c. Then again the *Tuſcans*, and indeed the *Italians* of almoſt every other State, pronounce the *ci* and *ce*, as we ſhould by putting an *b* betwixt the initial and final letters, as in the words *chirp* and *cheſs*; but a *Venetian* has not the power of expreƈtng thoſe words, otherwiſe than *ſirp* and *ſeſs*. Were the *Venetians*,

tians, for the prefervation of their lives, put to the teſt of pronouncing the word *Chibboleth*, as the *Ephramites*, at the paſſage of the river *Jordan*, were to the teſt of the word *Shibboleth*, like them, they would every man periſh; for they could only utter *Sibboleth*.

If this ſtricture on their language be a little too bold, I may venture at leaſt to take ſome freedoms with the indecorum of their bar. I ſhall not enter into the particulars of the extraordinary forms of their narrators, their interruptors, &c. a noiſy, uncivilifed manner of pleading; but ſhall only deſcribe, if I am able, the agitation and fury of the pleaders, more like that of a *Demoniac*, than of a man endeavouring, by ſound reaſon, to convince the judges and the audience of the juſtice of his client's cauſe. Every advocate mounts into a ſmall pulpit, a little elevated above the audience, where he opens his harangue with ſome gentleneſs, but does not long contain himſelf within thoſe limits; his voice ſoon cracks, and, what is very remarkable, the beginning of moſt ſentences (whilſt he is under any agitation, or ſeeming enthuſiaſm, in pleading) is at a pitch above his natural voice, ſo as to occaſion a wonderful diſcord:

cord: then, if he mean to be very emphatical, he strikes the pulpit with his hands five or six times together, as quick as thought, stamping at the same time, so as to make the great room resound with this species of oratory; at length, in the fury of his argument, he descends from the pulpit, runs about pleading on the floor, returns in a violent passion back again to the pulpit, thwacks it with his hands more than at first, and continues in this rage, running up and down the pulpit several times, till he has finished his harangue. They seem to be in continual danger of dropping their wiggs from their heads, and I am told it sometimes happens. The audience smile now and then at this extraordinary behaviour; but were a counsellor to plead in this manner at *Westminster*, his friends would certainly send for a *Bedlam* doctor. I take it for granted there may be some few who speak with more dignity; but the advocates I saw, were all men of eminence in their profession; and believe me, when I assure you, that the account I have here given of the usage of the Bar, is exact and simple, though it may seem to favour of extravagance.

I am, Sir, &c.

LETTER IX.

PADUA, *Sept.* 1765.

SIR,

THIS State continues to encourage private informations. There are about the Doge's palace a great number of small lyon's heads in the walls, large enough to receive into their mouths a letter or billet: Over the heads are labels, pointing out what the nature of the information should be; some of them direct the accusation to be against this or that kind of contraband; others against different species of crimes, and so on. As all men know these clandestine informers are sure of secrecy and a reward from the state, it renders every illegal act, which requires accomplices, extremely dangerous; but the practice has a terrible tendency to corrupt the heart of man, and make him sacrifice his friendships and benefactors to the lust of gain.

The Doge's station is not so enviable as may be imagined, and many accept of the dignity rather for the honour of their families and posterity, than to gratify their own inclination;

nation; for, in general, they are chosen from some high office, which they can hold compatibly with the enjoyment of a sociable life; but the moment they become a Doge, they are to avoid all show of equality and familiarity, and must, in a manner, seclude themselves from the sweets of society: Besides, the office is laborious, and a Doge has not pre-eminence enough above the other nobles, to render the bitter draught palatable.

The common people flatter themselves they are the freest state in *Europe*; and the nasty fellows esteem it a proof they are so, that they can let down their breeches where-ever, and before whomsoever they please; accordingly all St *Mark's-Place*, and many parts of that sumptuous marble building, the Doge's palace, are dedicated to *Cloacina*, and you may see the votaries at their devotions every hour of the day, as much whilst the Nobles are going in, and coming out, as at any other time.

This morning we arrived at *Padua*, in our way to *Bologna*. A second and more perfect view of the palaces on the banks of the *Brenta*, heightened our opinion of them, particularly of that belonging to *Pisani*, which is

truly

truly magnificent: The gardens are likewise noble, but laid out in a taste long since discarded in *England*, namely, in a variety of plots filled either with sand, or long unmowed grass, and bordered with box, &c.

The second visit to *Padua* has made the same impression on me as the first, leaving a melancholy on the mind, to see a city so noble and renowned in ancient days, so depopulated and impoverished as it now is. They have a fair which lasts from about the middle of *June* to the middle of *July*, and is their greatest harvest; for during that time, they have a fine Opera, and it is the custom of the rich *Venetians* to come and pass that month there. Many *Venetians* have houses at *Padua*, which are shut up all the rest of the year. It is not only *Padua*, but every other town in the territory of the republick, that appears poor in comparison of the mother city. It is said that the Senate of *Venice* treats her subjects with great partiality, discouraging every invention or manufacture, though it should be for the good of the whole, if it clash with the immediate benefit of *Venice* itself. It is to be remembered, that the Republick of *Venice* was originally nothing more than the city of of *Venice*; it was by conquest that she acquired territory, and added other cities to this capital; it is no wonder, therefore, if she retain some predilection.

I am, Sir, &c.

LETTER X.

LORETTO, *Oct.* 1765.

SIR,

WE are arrived at *Loretto*, through the most fertile and best inhabited countries of the Ecclesiastical State. We have passed *Bologna, Immola, Faenza, Forli, Cefanea, Rimini, Cattolico, Pesaro, Fano, Sinigaglia,* and *Ancona.* Because I will not tire you with accounts of things to be found in books, unless I am particularly struck by them, I have forborne to enter into any detail of the most venerable remain of antiquity in the world, I mean the amphitheatre at *Verona*; nor have I spoken of the excellent works of *Palladio,* at *Vicenza*, particularly the Olympic Theatre. I have said nothing of the institute,

or

or Musæum at *Bologna*, and the collection of pictures in that city, which is esteemed the second or third in *Italy*. I might have expatiated on the bridge at *Rimini*, built in the *Augustan* age, which is wonderfully preserved, and is so beautiful, that it is said *Palladio* declared he could not improve upon it. I confess I could not behold this bridge, and the triumphal arch of *Cæsar* in the same town, without great pleasure; but what crowned that day's journey was the passage of the celebrated antient *Rubicon*: I shall just observe on *Sinigaglia*, that it seems to be the only rising town in *Italy*: The occasion of this flourishing condition of a town in the Pope's dominions, is, the vogue of a fair, once a year, which is annually improving, and draws such a concourse of people from distant countries, as, with time, will enrich this district,

Ancona is one of the most striking prospects in *Italy*; it stands both on the summit and the brow of a hill. It has a mole, a fine citadel, and, in short, is a flourishing town, when considered under the disadvantages that every place labours here, from the infinite concessions that are made to the church, both by the commercial and the military parts of the nation.

nation. It is hardly to be expressed how beautiful the neighbouring districts of *Ancona* are; the road is hilly, but the gradual wavings of the vineyards, and arable grounds, afford the most pleasing images I have seen of Peace and Plenty. The *Adriatick* near the road, on one side, and the *Appenines*, at the distance, perhaps, of thirty miles, on the other, serve to beautify the prospect.

This morning we visited our Lady of *Loretto*, in her *Santa Casa* (Holy House.) The church, and the porticos leading to it, make a good appearance, and the inside of the church would be thought very handsome in *England*. The *Santa Casa* is an oblong square room, and, to the best of my judgment, of about thirty three feet by fifteen, the walls of which are ordinary brick, but by the care of *Sixtus Quintus*, and other Popes, the four sides were surrounded with marble, on which *Michael Angelo*, and his rival cotemporaries, have lavished all their skill in the sculpture. The good people tell you, that care was taken not to give any support to the walls, lest the Virgin should have been offended at the presumption; for they believe that every part of the *Santa Casa* is durable to all eternity, and
refer

refer you to the marble steps, and a brazen Bas Relief of our Saviour; the first of which have deep impressions made by the Pilgrims, who walk round the *Santa Casa* on their knees, and the other is almost worn out by the kisses of devout Christians; whilst, say they, there is not the least symptom of decay from use, in the threshold of the *Santa Casa*, though trodden every day by many thousands.

Our Lady of *Loretto* has a black face, and is ornamented with an infinity of rich jewels. She is lodged in a sanctuary; for the room is divided into two apartments, and the walls of that in which she is lodged, are lined with gold. Under the image is the *Camino Santo*, or Holy Chimney. They are continually saying Mass before her; and, indeed, the resort of Pilgrims and Votaries is so great, that they say in the whole church about two hundred Masses every day. Last *Saturday* and *Sunday* many thousand communicants received the Sacrament each day, as they tell us.

The Treasury of our Lady is not open every hour of the day, as the *Santa Casa* is. We waited till about ten o'clock, when we were admitted gratis, with the other expectants, who were all, except one Gentleman and Lady,

LETTER X.

Lady, peasants and poor folks. The treasures are ranged all along one side of a handsome room, and contained within folding doors. They are donatives from all the Princes of *Europe*, and others, who have wished to make their court to our Lady, infinitely exceeding in value what the most sanguine visitors suppose.

I presume you have read the history of the several migrations of the holy house; but as it may possibly have escaped your memory, I will give you a short account of them from the Legend. This small tenement is supposed to have been inhabited by the Virgin Mary, and for some wise purpose was brought by an Angel from the Holy Land to *Dalmatia* in 1291, where, not being received with due respect, it was carried in 1294 into the district of *Recanati*; but this situation favouring the concealment of robbers and assassins, who infested that road, it was again removed to within a hundred paces of the town of *Recanati*; and here new reasons arising for another removal, it was carried to the place where it now stands. The Lady who was proprietor of the ground, to which the house was first brought, being named *Lauretta*, gave it the name it now bears. It

It appears wonderful to me, that some *Corsair*, with a hundred and fifty, or two hundred men, should not attempt to surprize and plunder this church. A *coup-de-Main*, well managed, I think, would succeed. There are about thirty soldiers in the town, to defend it in case of an attack; but, I suppose, they, as well as the Monks, and common people, believing that the Virgin requires no assistance, would instantly take to their heels; they do not, however, live under the least apprehension of danger. Every body in that country still tells a story how the *Turks* have more than once undertaken the enterprize, but have immediately retired, upon finding that the Blessed Virgin threw a cloud before their eyes, and obstructed their farther progress; and they are now persuaded they will never more revisit them. However, if a resolute *Italian* renegado, who knew the town, were to land a crew of brave Mahometans in the night, I do not doubt but the Virgin, with all her miraculous powers, would yield to the Turban, and take a trip to *Barbary*.

Their annals inform us, that two or three experiments have been made by the Pope's permission, of removing a stone, or a piece of wood

wood from the holy chappel; but the possessors, though they received it for a holy purpose, have found themselves under the necessity of restoring it, in order to pacify the Blessed Virgin; as they always felt themselves unhappy, either in body or mind, so long as the *Santa Casa* remained dismantled.

I am, Sir, &c.

LETTER XI.

ROME, *Oct.* 1765.

SIR,

WE arrived at this place, after a journey of seven days, with accommodations uncomfortable enough. Give what scope you please to your fancy, you will never imagine half the disagreeableness that *Italian* beds, *Italian* cooks, *Italian* post-horses, *Italian* postilions, and *Italian* nastiness, offer to an *Englishman*, in an autumnal journey; much more to an *English* woman.

At *Turin, Milan, Venice, Rome*, and, perhaps, two or three other towns, you meet with good accommodation; but no words can express the wretchedness of the other inns.

No other bed than one of straw, with a matrafs of straw, and next to that a dirty sheet, sprinkled with water, and, consequently, damp; for a covering you have another sheet, as coarse as the first, and as coarse as one of our kitchen jack-towels, with a dirty coverlet. The bedsted consists of four wooden forms, or benches: An *English* Peer and Peeress must lye in this manner, unless they carry an upholsterer's shop with them, which is very troublesome. There are, by the bye, no such things as curtains, and hardly, from *Venice* to *Rome*, that cleanly and most useful invention, a privy; so that what should be collected and buried in oblivion, is for ever under your nose and eyes. Take along with you, that in all these inns the walls are bare, and the floor has never once been washed since it was first laid. One of the most indelicate customs here, is, that men, and not women, make the ladies beds, and would do every office of a maid servant, if suffered. To sum up, in a word, the total of *Italian* nastiness, your chamber, which you would wish to be the sweetest, is by far the most offensive room in the house, for reasons I shall not explain. I must tell you, that they never scour their pewter, and unless you were

to

to see it, you will not conceive how dirty and nauseous it grows in thirty or forty years. Their knives are of the same colour as their pewter, and their table-cloths and napkins such as you see on joint-stools in *Bartholomew-Fair*, where the mob eat their sausages. In these inns they make you pay largely, so much a head, and send up ten times as much as you can eat. For example, this is almost constantly the fare.—A soop like wash, with pieces of liver swimming in it; a plate full of brains, fried in the shape of fritters; a dish of livers and gizzards; a couple of fowls (always killed after your arrival) boiled to rags, without any the least kind of sauce, or herbage; another fowl, just killed, stewed as they call it; then two more fowls, or a turkey roasted to rags. I must not omit to mention, that all over *Italy*, I mean on their roads, the chickens and fowls are so stringy, you may divide the breast into as many filaments as you can a halfpenny-worth of thread. Now and then we get a little piece of mutton, or veal, and generally speaking, it is the most eatable morsel that falls in our way. I should mention, that pigeons boiled and roasted, often supply the place of some of the above-mentioned dishes.

dishes. the bread all the way is exceedingly bad, and the butter so rancid, it cannot be touch'd, or even borne within the reach of our smell. We procured the other day, a pint of cream, and made a little extempore butter, which proved almost as good as any we eat in *England*, so that the fault seems to lye in the manufacture, and not in the milk; yet such is the force of education and custom, that the people here do not wish to have it better than it is. In *Savoy*, amongst the *Alps*, we were often astonished at the excellence of their diet; so great is the disparity betwixt *French* and *Italian* cooks, on the *Savoy* and the *Loretto* roads.

But what is a greater evil to travellers than any of the above recited, though not peculiar to the *Loretto* road, is the infinite number of gnats, bugs, fleas, and lice, which infest us by night and by day.

You will grant, after this description of the horrors of an *Italian* journey, that one ought to take no small pleasure in treading on classic ground; yet, believe me, I have not caricatured; every article of it is literally true. If the subject of this Letter be disgustful, comfort yourself, that I shall seldom or never touch upon it more, during my absence.

I am, Sir, &c.

LETTER XII.

Rome, *Oct.* 1765.

SIR,

I Should not have closed the account of my journey to *Rome*, without mentioning a few more particulars. When you are in the neighbourhood of *Ancona*, were you not to behold the extreme wretchedness of the inhabitants, you would think yourself from the aspect of the country in the most opulent kingdom of the world: The towns all placed on eminencies, look beautiful at a distance, and would be much admired were they never approached. Betwixt *Macerata* and *Tolentino* by the side of the road, there are the remains of a large amphitheatre, which amongst a thousand other indications, prove how populous that district must have been, where now we did not see a hut. I cannot say the passage of the *Alps* had absolutely inured me to that of the *Apennines*; some precipices here are so lofty, that whoever is terrified at the *Alps*, should never pass the *Apennines* for pleasure.

There has fallen this laſt year, prodigious quantities of rain, which have carried away many bridges, broken down ſeveral banks, and very much overflowed the country: Neverthelefs the rivers near the mountains ſoon empty themſelves into the diſtant rivers, driving before them great quantities of dirt and mud, which have been waſhed from the mountains; it is this dirt and mud, which, in the courſe of a few ages, choak up certain rivers of *Italy*; and the waters ſeeking new beds, produce a total alteration in the face of the country. Betwixt *Padua* and *Roverigo* you ſee one great branch of the *Po*, quite deſerted by its waters, and I ſuppoſe it was the revolution produced by this accident that was the ſubject of an expenſive law-ſuit, which I heard tried at *Venice* for an eſtate of about ſix thouſand pounds a year ſterling: The matter in conteſt was this: About fifty years ſince, the banks of one branch of the *Po* giving way, the water took another courſe, and overflowed the neighbouring diſtricts; but the revulſion was ſo great, as to expoſe and lay dry a large extent of marſhy ground, which is now worth annually the above ſum. The queſtion in diſpute, is the title to the

drained

LETTER XII.

drained ground. This grand cause was to have been finally heard by the court of forty, one of the days that I attended their pleadings: The suit had been carried on at an incredible expence during forty years, and now upon a division of the judges, there were seventeen for the plaintiff, and seventeen for the defendant, two judges not voting, the other four being absent. The form of the state admitted of a second hearing before the same court, the ensuing day, but unhappily their voices again were equal, and, now the parties must renew the whole process, and be led through all their courts again, perhaps for the space of another forty years.

We passed the *Campania* of *Rome*, the unwholesomeness of which is held in such horror by the *Romans*, that no foreigner, nor any *Italian*, if he can possibly avoid it, lies on the road there. Accordingly it will be conceived, that their is very indifferent accommodation in the *Campania*, on which account, we found it necessary to keep our post-horses all night at a shabby inn, half way to the post-house before you arrive at the *Campania*, as preferring dirty beds and dirty provisions, to no beds, no provisions, and a supposed pestilential climate. The

Romans when they travel poſt on this road, uſually ſet out from *Rome* early enough to reach *Terni* the firſt evening; or, if they muſt lye one night in the *Campania*, when the days are ſhort, it is at *Caſtel-Nuovo*, a little above thirty miles from *Rome*. It grieves one to behold ſo fine a country as the *Campania* might be made, by a plentiful population, now almoſt a waſte and barren deſart. There is a part of the road within twenty miles of *Rome* exceedingly well paved with large ſtones of flat ſurfaces; but the graſs riſes in their interſtices; ſo little is now trodden that path which leads to the city of *Rome*, once ſo mighty, ſo populous, and ſo frequented.

I am, Sir, &c.

LETTER XIII.

ROME, *Oct.* 1765.

SIR,

A MAN, on his firſt arrival at *Rome*, is not much fired with its appearance; the narrowneſs of the ſtreets, the thinneſs of the inhabitants, the prodigious quantity of
Monks

LETTER XIII.

Monks and beggars, give but a gloomy aspect to this renowned city. There are no rich tradesmen here, who, by their acquisitions, either enoble their sons, or marry their daughters into the houses of princes. All the shops seem empty, and the shop-keepers poor; not one hackney coach in so large a town, a notable proof there is no middle station betwixt those who always ride, and those who always walk. This is the first impression; but turn your eye from that point of view, to the magnificence of their churches, to the venerable remains of ancient *Rome*, to the prodigious collection of pictures and antique statues, to the very river and ground itself, formerly the habitation of that people, which, from our cradles, we have been taught to adore, and, with a very few grains of enthusiasm in your composition, you will feel more than satisfied.

The surface of modern *Rome* is certainly more elevated than it was in antient times; such an alteration must happen, in the course of ages, to every city which has been often destroyed by time and fire, as all the rubbish is seldom removed; but the antient pavement, on which *Trajan*'s pillar stands, shews the elevation in that place not to be above seven or eight feet; and, I am informed, some of the triumphal arches are not above three or four feet in the ground. The *Tarpeian* rock is still of such a height, that should a man be thrown from it, his bones would be in the greatest danger, though there would be no certainty of breaking his neck; nor, indeed, would it be certain, though the rock were ten or fifteen feet higher, as some have supposed it in the time of the *Romans* when this kind of execution was in vogue: I should imagine, therefore, they had some method of dispatching the delinquent, when death did not immediately ensue from the fall; perhaps an executioner was at the foot of the rock, ready for this purpose in case of that event, which, I imagine, would often happen, though the rock had been of twice its present height. Men, in falling from high places, are sometimes killed on the spot, but more frequently languish a considerable time before death. I conclude, therefore, that there is no greater alteration in the site of *Rome* than what I have mentioned. The most remarkable change is this, that the *Campus Martius* was, in the time of the

antient

antient *Romans*, an open area, and now it is covered with houses. The circuit of the city, in *Pliny*'s time, did not, by his account, exceed the present dimensions, but its populousness must have been amazingly different.

Were an antiquarian to lament over any fall, any metamorphosis of antient *Rome*, perhaps it might be the present state of the *Forum*, where, now, there is every *Thursday* and *Friday*, a market for cows and oxen, on the very spot where the *Roman* orators were accustomed to thunder out their eloquence in the cause of their clients, their country, and their gods: Accordingly, the *Forum* now is known by the name of *Campo Vaccino*.

Surrounding the *Forum* are many vestiges of antique grandeur; triumphal arches; remains of temples; the ruins of the Imperial Palace; the *Campidoglio*, &c. all bespeaking the magnificent state of *Rome* in the times of the Emperors. The great Amphitheatre, called also *Il Coloſſeo*, where the spectacle of combats was exhibited, is also in its neighbourhood. In this place the spirit of modern *Rome* seems to prevail over that of antient *Rome*; for where the wild beasts and gladiators formerly entertained seventy or eighty thou-

thousand spectators, you now see a few miserable old women and beggars, who are praying at the feet of fourteen small chapels, which represent the fourteen mysteries of our Saviour's passion.

I am, dear Sir, &c.

LETTER XIV.

ROME, *October* 1765.

SIR,

ONE of the most curious arts of modern *Rome*, is the *Mosaick* work carried on in St *Peter*'s church, which they are now cultivating at an expence beyond the reach of a private purse. I am not to tell you the invention is antient, and has always continued in use; but it has been so little practised till within the present century, that it appears almost a discovery. It is a method by which the capital pictures of the great masters will be transmitted to posterity in great perfection. The manner of working in *Mosaick*, you will, I hope, conceive, from the following superficial description.

The

LETTER XIV.

The artists, by the means of fire, compose a cake of a nature betwixt stone and glass, but not in the least transparent; it is as hard and durable as marble, and they have the skill to stain it with a colour of what shade they please, which they so fix by the fire, that it preserves its liveliness for ever. They manufacture as great a variety of these coloured stones, as will answer to the different tints of any picture. The artificial stone is brittle, and the workmen acquire, from use, the dexterity of chipping off at a stroke, with a proper instrument, pieces of the shape and size they wish, some exceedingly small, but, generally speaking, nearly square, and from two or three lines to half an inch broad; nevertheless, as the thickness of the cake is often near an inch, the shape of the pieces chipped off will be an oblong square, and may be aptly enough compared to a double or treble cube. The workmen have an infinite variety of these differently coloured pieces of stone, placed in different cells of a drawer; these lie within their reach, whilst they are composing the picture, and they select the proper coloured pieces of stone, as a compositor does the types when he is setting the press.

That

That the *Mosaick*, in very large pictures, may not be subject either to fall in, or bulge out, they made the back, or slab, of several pieces of flat stones, cramped together with iron: these stones are of a very hard nature, and are also extremely thick, in order to render them still less liable to warp. They unite as many of these flat stones to each other as will equal the size of the picture they are to copy. On this slab, or frame, they lay a particular paste, or cement, which, in a short time, becomes almost as hard as marble; but, whilst it remains in a state of softness, they apply the *Mosaick* work, striking into the cement with a gentle stroke of a small hammer, the little oblong pieces of stone, of such tints, as will represent the part they are to imitate. They lay but little of the cement at a time, lest it should grow hard too suddenly. This process goes on so very slowly, that ten or eleven men working on the famous picture of the Transfiguration, by *Raphael*, require eight or nine years to finish it; when compleated, it will cost about three thousand pounds sterl.

When they have covered the cement entirely, the work appears extremely rude; the workmen, therefore, wait till the cement has acquired

LETTER XIV.

acquired the hardnefs of ftone, and that its coalition with the *Mofaick* is perfect, when they rub down and polifh the furface, after which it affumes a wonderful beauty, though it must be confeffed, it is not equal to the painting on canvafs; for, in fome lights, you fee not only a gloffinefs, but even the cracks in the *Mofaick*. The copy, however, in *Mofaick*, of the celebrated St *Michael* of *Guido*, looks almoft as well as the original. It is unqueftionable that the artifts improve daily; for I obferve that the late works greatly excel thofe done fome years fince, which, on a clofe infpection, appear in certain places uneven and coarfe, and make you regret the original.

The Connoiffeur, or, indeed, any man who has a relifh for the fine arts, muft be delighted on this occafion, to reflect, that the example of fuch wonderful excellence will now be preferved, to excite the emulation of the fame kind of geniufes, fhould the world once more produce fuch a clafs; or, to fpeak in the language of the painters, fuch a fchool of men.

I might have taken notice, that the artifts do not work from the original, but from a copy, which is another article of great expence, as it is neceffary the copy fhould be a
good

good one. I had imagined the sole reason for employing a copy was to obviate the danger of injuring the original; but they say, as the colours of the copy are fresh, they can imitate them better than from an original, where they are by time become faded and dead. I have mentioned that the antients used *Mosaicks*, but they had not the art of making and staining stone; they used only natural marble, &c. which did not furnish them with the same quantity of shades the moderns are possessed of, and, consequently, their colouring was less perfect.

 The *Mosaick* of *Florence* is not unlike that of the antients: It is composed of a great variety of differently coloured marbles, flints, stones, &c. The workmen are obliged to saw off every little piece, which demands much more time than the method of chipping them off, as practised in the *Roman Mosaick*, and, therefore, the *Florentine* is still much dearer than the *Roman*; indeed a large picture would amount to an incredible sum: On this account they confine their work to small pictures, tables, &c. which, after all, notwithstanding the great expence, are by no means so beautiful as the *Roman Mosaick* pictures. *I am, &c.*

LETTER. XV.

Rome, *Oct.* 1765.

SIR,

IT would be idle, and contrary to my declared plan of writing, should I attempt any description of the celebrated pictures, or statues at *Rome*; I shall therefore only beg leave to observe, from my own feeling, that, in the midst of all this excellence, the dying Gladiator affects me most. The *Farnese Hercules* is in the highest reputation, as an exquisite performance, and would indeed have been a fine piece of sculpture, had there been such an original in nature; but, as I happen to know, from my particular studies, that some certain muscles of a man's body, however much inflated, would not assume the shape they do here, I cannot be pleased, as most men are, with the *Farnese Hercules*; on the contrary, all is nature in the dying Gladiator, and, indeed, the expression is so strong, a man may walk round and round the statue till he almost forget it is stone.

LETTER XV.

The magnificence of the *Roman* Emperors, in embellishing the city, rose to such a height, that they ransacked all the quarries of *Egypt*, for alabaster, granite, porphyry, and every kind of marble that country afforded; and, though time and gothic rage must have destroyed great quantities, yet, such was the profusion brought to *Rome*, that, besides the amazing numbers of columns, statues, vases, and tables, still preserved intire, you see the very posts in the streets, all of them without exception, made of granite, alabaster, or marble; but the most stupendous sights of all, are the monstrous obelisks, consisting of only one piece of marble. I meditate on these objects till I am lost in wonder and confusion. We have no idea of the mechanical powers by which they were dug out of the quarry, and brought from *Egypt*: We are astonished at the enormous size of the stones at *Stonehenge*, and cannot comprehend by what contrivance they were carried and laid in that form; but the largest of them is small, compared with the largest obelisk at *Rome*, which I think is a hundred & one feet long, and proportionably thick.

The ruin of the triumphal bridge near St *Angelo*, is an object that cannot but strike a

man

man of letters: This was the bridge over which every General marched into the city, to whom a triumph was decreed, either for the conqueſt of a province, or any other ſignal victory. From the time of *Romulus*, to that of the Emperor *Probus*, there were about three hundred and twenty of theſe triumphs. There are now only a few remains of the piers. Who can behold this ſcene, without ruminating on the nature of the human heart, and recollecting to what trials it muſt have been expoſed in the courſe of ſo proud and ſo flattering a proceſſion?

Many of the churches in this city, and above all St *Peter*'s, are ſo very magnificent, that they vie with ancient *Rome* in every article but that of durableneſs, much of their beauty being derived from pictures, ſtucco, and gilding, the tranſitory ornaments of two or three ages. I cannot forbear remarking, in this place, that the pride of modern *Rome* is one of the cauſes of her wretchedneſs: She boaſts of her gold and ſilver lying dead in her churches; but had that gold and ſilver a free circulation through the country, it would enliven trade, and furniſh property to thousands who are now starving in the most pressing indigence.

St *Peter*'s never fails to please both the learned and the unlearned eye; the wonderful regularity and adjustment of its parts, like the beauty of a fine face, demand no skill in drawing to taste its charms: Then its colonades, fountains, and obelisk, give it an inimitable elegance. It must be confessed, however, that the approach to this noble edifice, is confined and shabby; but they now talk of demolishing the narrow mean street leading from St *Angelo*; and should this design take place, the avenue will be answerable to the building; though, to render St *Peter's* church still more perfect, the *Vatican*, with its eleven thousand chambers, should be removed, which, like an ugly excrescence, protuberates on one side; and destroys the symmetry of the elevation.

In the *Vatican*, besides a great number of *Raphael*'s paintings, are the excellent and celebrated statues of the *Belvedere Apollo*, the *Laocoon*, and the *Antinous*. The *Laocoon* wants an arm: There lyes on the ground one of marble, which, it is said, *Michael Angelo* had begun, in order to perfect

the

the ſtatue, but, perceiving how unſpirited his work would appear, compared with the original, he left the limb in the ſtate we ſee it, not half executed, a monument of his modeſty and ſelf-knowledge. It may be imagined that no one ſince, has been ſo preſumptuous to make an attempt after him, and therefore the deficiency is ſupplied by an arm of *terra cuota.*

I am, Sir, &c.

LETTER XVI.

NAPLES, *Nov.* 1765.

SIR,

THE road from *Rome* to this place is bad enough, the inns are ſtill worſe; nay worſe than thoſe on the *Loretto* road; for, in the town of *Loretto,* there was good accommodation, but all the way to *Naples* we never once crept within the ſheets, not daring to encounter the vermin and naſtineſs of thoſe beds. I attempted to pleaſe myſelf with the conceit of travelling the ſame road that *Horace* did in his journey to *Brunduſium*; but my ſenſations were too ſtrong for my fancy. The swampy soil and marshes on the right hand, with a string of barren mountains on the left, for scores of miles together, may amuse, but cannot delight a traveller. Did we not know that ancient *Italy* was much more populous than it now is; did we not know that popolousness renders a country rich and chearful, I should have suspected those masters of the universe had, in their haughtiness, and from a contempt of all other nations, called theirs the Garden of the World; for, beautiful and fertile as some parts of it are, the amazing quantity of barren mountains, extending from almost the one extremity to the other, should seem to deprive it of that character; and, however bold and uncommon the assertion may appear, I think *England* a better resemblance of a garden than *Italy*; and should not hesitate to oppose our verdure and inclosures, to their myrtle and orange trees, which last, by the bye, are not to be seen in winter out of green-houses, except in the southern parts of *Italy*.

Whilst I was in *England*, I never heard the words northern climate pronounced, but they conveyed to me an idea of barrenness and imperfection. I had always conceived, that vegetables

LETTER XVI.

vegetables and garden fruits attained a flavour and favourinefs in the more Southern Climes, unknown to the latitude of 51; but, to my great furprize, I do not find that any of their herbage is equal, in tafte and fweetnefs, to that which grows in our gardens; their green pea is far lefs delicious than ours; befides (if I am rightly informed) they have but one fort of green pea; then what is ftill more furprifing, few of their fruits excell ours; I believe none, except their water-melons, their grapes, and their figs: An *Englifh* Gentleman of diftinction, in this place, with the rafberry-jam he imports from *England*, makes iced rafberry of a much higher flavour than any we meet with at *Naples* made immediately from the fruit itfelf. If they have not peaches to be compared with ours, and no nectarines, I prefume it is owing to the violence of the fummer fun, though poffibly thefe defects may arife from their ignorance of cultivation in *Italy*. A certain Noble of *Venice*, well known in the polite world for his attachment to the fine arts, has procured a fkilful gardener from *England* within thefe few years, in hopes of improving the culture of his garden. I converfed with this gardener, whom I found under a ſtate of diſcouragement and deſpair. He told me he had not yet ever taſted a peach in *Italy* of a true flavour, and he believed he never ſhould, for that he was thwarted and obſtructed by the other gardeners, in his attempts to reform their practice, and that he had no authority over them, but was confined to his own proper departments, which he told me would anſwer very little purpoſe.

From *Capua* (about four miles from the ruins of the ancient *Capua*) the road to *Naples* is very pleaſant; the gardens and vineyards on each ſide are well cultivated; however, the diſtrict of *Capua* does not anſwer the idea we have of its luxury in the times of *Hannibal*, if I may judge from the great difficulty I found of procuring a morſel of dinner in that town.

I am, Sir, &c.

LETTER XVII.

NAPLES *Nov.* 1765.

SIR,

AFTER an absence of some months, I am persuaded you will be pleased to hear from your old friend and acquaintance; and, therefore, I shall not surfeit you with nauseous apologies for the trouble I give you. I take it for granted, Mr —— has communicated some part of my correspondence, as he tells me you shuddered at our passage over the *Alps*. I know your aversion to altitudes, and conceive you would be giddy, if not terrified, in looking down such perpendicular depths and precipices. Some parts of the *Alps* exhibit a most delightful and tremendous prospect, and were the first great object I met with amongst the *marvellous*. I think the city of *Venice* floating on the water, with its beautiful adjacent islands, may be ranked as the second; and I will venture to mention St. *Peter*'s as the third, though it partake not of beauties derived from Nature, being a meer work of Art; but, above all, I admire the heavens,

heavens, the earth, and the sea of *Naples*. The islands, the mountains, the Bay, the buildings, and the slope on which the buildings stand, render the view of this city enchantingly pretty. I am lodged on the brink of the Bay, with a beautiful winding coast, the celebrated island *Caprea*, and the more celebrated Mount *Vesuvius* before my eyes. Since my arrival we have had blustering weather, and, though in *November*, more thunder and lightening than I ever knew in *July* in our latitudes; but the sea is so sheltered that there is no horror in the scene, and the streets are so well paved, that they become clean and dry in a few hours after a deluge. I can imagine, and am told, that the heats of summer are dreadful, but, thank God, they are not to be my concern; I am to enjoy the sweets only of a *Neapolitan* winter, and, as far as I can judge, they are unspeakable to a man who suffers in his lungs from moisture and cold. Damps are little known in this place, neither furniture nor walls are much injured by that circumstance; and for temperature of the air, suffice it to inform you, that, in order to write this letter comfortably, I chuse to open the windows. Could an

asthmatic

asthmatic man jump from *London* to the lodgings I have taken, though at any risk of his neck, he would do well to venture; but I cannot say it would be worth while to go and return as we do, through so much filth, and so many sufferings from bugs, lice, fleas, gnats, spiders, &c.

Rome gave me much entertainment, and I propose to make it another visit; could I stay there four or five months, I should certainly run over all the classics, and compare the objects with the descriptions. If a man have no taste, not to say a little enthusiasm for the antiquities and glory of antient *Rome*, I do not know a more melancholy place than modern *Rome*. Indeed, the excellent pictures to be seen in their churches and palaces, are ambrosia to some palates; but, I confess, that after having paid my respects to fifty thousand of them, I am satiated, and grow indifferent in my visits to the second fifty thousand. One sees too quick a succession to be much gratified; a man has not time to contemplate, and fix in his memory the several characteristicks of the different masters, and I question whether I should not have had much more pleasure in seeing twelve or fifteen only, of the first

pieces,

pieces, than that infinite quantity which has paſſed ſo rapidly in review before my eyes. The churches at *Rome* are ſo ſplendid and rich, that they have deſtroyed my appetite for that purſuit too; beſides, to uſe a metaphyſical expreſſion, the aſſociation of ideas ſpoils my reliſh for theſe gaudy and ſumptuous objects, as I cannot look on their golden altars, and their fat prieſts, without reflecting on their deſerted *Campania*, and ſtarving laity; however I muſt mention, that as all ranks of men are allowed to wear a churchman's habit, and many do, a ſtranger is not to imagine that every perſon he ſees with a band, *&c.* is an Eccleſiaſtick: there are multitudes in this dreſs at *Rome*, who have not the leaſt connection with the church.

The Pope is ſaid to be a good natured old man, and, I think, I can read that character in his countenance and geſtures: When he returned to *Rome* for the winter, from his palace in the country, my company and I met him in the ſkirts of the town, and having no ſcruples of conſcience to pay the ſame devoirs that others do here to a Prince of the country, and the head of the church, we threw ourſelves on our knees, evidently to his

his great satisfaction; for, I assure you his eyes sparkled. We made a small groupe at a distance from any croud: I could see he was gathering himself into an attitude to give us an extraordinary benediction as he approached us, perceiving we were *English*; and I flatter myself to this moment, that he felt an inward joy, when he extended his hands, and poured out the blessing on so many wretched Hereticks. I will not say we are the better for his Holiness, but, to use the Catholick argument, we are certainly not the worse.

I am, Sir, &c.

LETTER XVIII.

NAPLES, *Nov.* 1765.

SIR,

YOU tell me, two or three husbands are lately separated from their wives, and bemoan the degeneracy of the age in these instances. You suppose the manners of our people corrupted, because two or three married couple,

ple, either on the account of gallantry, or
averſion, have parted: With us here, it is
an argument of national virtue. We read
with aſtoniſhment that the examples are only
two or three in ſo large a kingdom. Were
Italians to ſeparate either on the account of
indifference or gallantry, there would be almoſt as many divorces as marriages. It appears to us, that, becauſe ſome ſeparate where
there is no affection, others may remain together becauſe there is affection; a paſſion
in a manner almoſt unknown betwixt huſbands and wives in this climate. When I
paſs ſo ſevere a cenſure on the ſtate of matrimony in theſe kingdoms, do not believe that
I ſpeak from a ſpirit of detraction, or without good grounds: I believe I can much
more ſatisfactorily ſolve this phænomenon,
than the ingenious *Monteſquieu* does that of the
different characters of different nations, from
the various latitudes in which they are ſitu-
ated, &c. How is it probable that huſbands
and wives ſhould have any eſteem, much
leſs love for each other, when they are always brought together without the leaſt par-
ticipation of their own; the fathers never
conſult the liking of the young people, but
look

look forwards to the endowments of the next generation, which are comprifed in two words, Fortune and Family. All that I have here faid is fo literally true, that it very feldom happens the parties know one another before the marriage articles are drawing up, and, perhaps, do not vifit twice, before the day of confummation; fhe, to that moment, is locked up in a convent.

Bad as the above fyftem is, it would not be fufficient to diffufe univerfal unhappinefs through the domains of *Hymen:* Chance and good fenfe would now and then render this fort of union agreeable, and even friendly; but that abominable and infernal fafhion of taking a Cicefbeo fo foon after they have quitted the altar, is a never failing meafure to eftrange whatever affection might otherwife have fprung up. Many people in *England* imagine the majority of Cicefbeos to be an innocent kind of dangling fribble; but they are utterly miftaken in the character; nor do I find it underftood here that the Ladies live in greater purity with their Cicefbeos than with their hufbands; and, generally fpeaking, with much lefs: If only one half of the Ladies practifed this cuftom, the other

half

half would defpife them; but, in fact, very few have any pretence to upbraid the reft with bad conduct, either from having no Cicefbeo, or living innocently with him: if there be any of the latter fort, their reward muft be in Heaven, or, Virtue muft be its own reward; as nobody gives them the leaft credit here for their continence, or fuppofes it practicable; nay, perhaps, they may laugh at it as ridiculous, fo pardonable and fo polite do they efteem this fpecies of immorality; and, to fay the truth, I myfelf have feen Princeffes, Dutcheffes, and their Cicefbeos, vifiting with the fame unconcernednefs, as an honeft citizen and his wife do; nor, after a little habit and ufe, do they afford me more matter of fpeculation. To give you an idea in one word, how much the mode of infeparablenefs betwixt them is eftablifhed, fuffice it to fay, that if you invite five ladies to dinner, you of courfe lay ten plates, as each for a certainty brings her Cicefbeo with her. You are not to imagine, that when I fpeak of an invitation of ladies, that a fingle woman is ever thought of; that charm in fociety, that innocence and fprightlinefs attendant upon youth, and the igno-

rance

rance of a deceitful world, is utterly unknown in *Italy*, nor are there more than two unmarried ladies in this metropolis, who visit; all the others are locked up in monasteries.

Children here have very little tendency to support the friendship and harmony of the married state; with us, the joint interest of both father and mother in their little ones, with perhaps the blended features they each discover in their progeny, do not contribute in a small degree to heal any accidental breaches, or at least, to make them live seemingly on good terms for the sake of their posterity. In *Italy*, a certain knowledge of every wife's attachment to a lover, extinguishes all social affection, and all fondness for the offspring; and it is only the eldest born, who the husband is sure belongs to him; and for that security, it is generally requisite, the birth should take place the first year, as the women seldom hold out longer without a Cicesbeo; indeed how should they? for a husband will not wait on his wife to a public place, and it is not the fashion for women to go, as in *England*, without men. I have been told, by a grave *Neapolitan* old Gentleman, the fault is entirely on the side of the husbands,

who

who are fickle from the nature of the climate, and cannot continue conftant to their wives many months, fo that the poor women are driven into this meafure; but, whether the practice arife from levity or compulfion, the confequence is dreadful to fociety, if there be any real delight, any charms in Virtue, and mutual Love.

Mr *Hamilton*, the Envoy, a very polite Gentleman, receives company every evening, which conduces much to the pleafure of the *Englifh* refiding here. It is the cuftom, when neither the Opera, nor any particular engagements prevent, to meet at his houfe, where we amufe ourfelves as we are difpofed, either at cards, the billiard-table, or his little concert; fome form themfelves into fmall parties of converfation, and as the members of this fociety are often Ambaffadors, Nuncios, Monfignoris, Envoys, Refidents, and the firft quality of *Naples*, you will conceive it to be inftructive as well as honourable.

I am, Sir, &c.

LETTER XIX.

NAPLES, *Nov.* 1765.

SIR,

A STRANGER, upon his arrival in so large and celebrated a city as *Naples*, generally makes the publick spectacles his first pursuit. These consist of the King's Theatre, where the serious Opera is performed, and of two smaller theatres, called *Theatro Nuovo*, and the *Theatro dei Fiorentini*, where they exhibit burlettas only. There is also a little dirty kind of a play-house, where they perform a comedy every night, though the Drama has so little encouragement at *Naples*, that their comedies are seldom frequented by any of the gentry, but seem to be chiefly an amusement for the populace, at least, that class of people just above the populace: However, I shall not fail to describe the present state of that stage, after having spoken of their Opera-houses.

The King's Theatre, upon the first view, is, perhaps, almost as remarkable an object as any a man sees in his travels: I not only speak from my own feeling, but the declaration of every foreigner here. The amazing extent of the ftage, with the prodigious circumference of the boxes, and height of the cieling, produce a marvellous effect on the mind, for a few moments; but the inftant the Opera opens, a fpectator laments this ftriking fight. He immediately perceives this ftructure does not gratify the ear, how much foever it may the eye. The voices are drowned in this immenfity of fpace, and even the orcheftra itfelf, though a numerous band, lies under a difadvantage: It is true, fome of the firft fingers may be heard, yet, upon the whole, it muft be admitted, that the houfe is better contrived to fee, than to hear an Opera.

There are fome who contend, that the fingers might be very well heard, if the audience were more filent; but it is fo much the fafhion at *Naples*, and, indeed, through all *Italy*, to confider the Opera as a place of rendezvous and vifiting, that they do not feem in the leaft to attend to the mufick, but laugh and talk through the whole performance, without any reftraint; and, it may be imagined, that an affembly of fo many hundreds converfing together fo loudly, muft entirely

cover

cover the voices of the singers. I was prepossessed of this custom before I left *England*, but had no idea it was carried to such an extreme. I had been informed, that though the *Italians* indulged this humour in some degree, yet, when a favourite song was singing, or the King was present, they observed a deep silence: I must, however, deny the fact in both cases, from what I have seen, though, possibly, they may have paid more regard to some songs, than to those I heard; and, probably, the audience may have shewn to Don *Carlos*, King of *Naples*, more respect than they do to his son, a youth of fifteen.

An *Englishman* wonders at this behaviour of the *Italians*; he comes with a notion that they are all enthusiastically fond of musick; that there is something in the climate which gives them this propensity, and that their natural genius is nursed and improved by a musical education: Upon enquiry, he finds his opinion almost groundless; very few Gentlemen here practise the fiddle, or any other instrument, and all the young Ladies are placed in convents, where they remain until they marry, or take the veil, and where musick is seldom a part of their education; nor can it be supposed that any woman, after marriage, undertakes so laborious a task as that of making a proficiency on the harpsichord: For these reasons, therefore, an *Italian* audience has no other pleasure in melody than what pure Nature affords; whereas, in *England*, the fine Ladies have also an acquired taste, the effect of assiduity and cultivation.

I cannot place the neglect of the study of musick amongst the Gentry of this country in a stronger light, than by mentioning, that I found it impossible, at *Venice* and here, to hire a harpsichord fit to play on; so small is the demand, I presume, for that instrument. Another argument how little musick is cultivated here, may be gathered from the circumstance of never printing their operas, or favourite airs, which would be a necessary consequence of a general demand, as we see is the case in *London* and *Paris*. By the bye, it may not be unworthy notice (to exemplify how necessary use is in every kind of exercise) that the greatest masters here, cannot play readily, at sight, a piece of printed musick. The reason they have assigned to me is, that printed notes are much closer to each other, than the written ones which they are accustomed

LETTER XIX.

tomed to. It will be natural, then, to afk, after this account, how it happens, that *Italy* furnifhes all *Europe* with muficians? The anfwer is, that the infinite quantity of mufic exhibited in their churches and chapels, provides bread, though the wages be fmall, for a prodigious number of performers; and, as trade is defpicable, and laborious employments are held in deteftation, parents are induced to bring up their children to this profeffion, which they can do at a fmall expence; for there are feveral hundred youths brought up to mufick, in their Confervatories, or charitable foundations: Now, where there are fo many hundreds in continual practice, it is not ftrange that emulation and genius fhould, every now and then, produce an excellent performer, who, if he be well advifed, will certainly fet out for *England*, where talents of every kind are rewarded ten-fold above what they are at *Naples*, except in the fingle inftance of the firft clafs of opera fingers, who are payed extravagantly, as I fhall explain in fome future letter.

I am, Sir, &c.

LETTER XX.

NAPLES, *Nov.* 1765.

SIR,

Notwithstanding the amazing noisiness of the audience, during the whole performance of the Opera, the moment the dances begin, there is a universal dead silence, which continues so long as the dances continue. Witty people, therefore, never fail to tell me, the *Neapolitans* go to *see*, not to *hear* an Opera. A stranger, who has a little compassion in his breast, feels for the poor singers, who are treated with so much indifference and contempt: He almost wonders that they can submit to so gross an affront; and I find, by their own confession, that however accustomed they be to it, the mortification is always dreadful, and they are eager to declare how happy they are when they sing in a country where more attention is paid to their talents.

One would suppose, from the regard shewn to the dances, that a superior excellence should be expected in this art; but *Naples* does not at present, afford any very capital performers,

nor

nor do the dances which have been brought on the stage this season, reflect much honour on their taste. They are, in general, exceedingly tedious, some lasting thirty-five minutes, and others twenty-five, with incidents and characters too vulgar and buffoonish; but it must be confessed that their scenery is extremely fine; their dresses are new and rich; and the musick is well adapted; but, above all, the stage is so large and noble, as to set off the performance to an inexpressible advantage.

The *Neapolitan* quality rarely dine or sup with one another, and many of them hardly ever visit, but at the Opera; on this account they seldom absent themselves, though the Opera be played three nights successively, and it be the same Opera, without any change, during ten or twelve weeks. It is customary for Gentleman to run about from box to box, betwixt the acts, and even in the midst of the performance; but the Ladies, after they are seated, never quit their box the whole evening. It is the fashion to make appointments for such and such nights. A Lady receives visitors in her box one night, and they remain with her the whole Opera; another night

she

she returns the visit in the same manner. In the intervals of the acts, principally betwixt the first and second, the proprietor of the box regales her company with iced fruits and sweet meats. I will soon take an opportunity of explaining to you what I mean by the proprietor of a box.

Besides the indulgence of a loud conversation, they sometimes form themselves into card parties; but, I believe, this custom does not prevail so much at present, as it did formerly, for I have never seen more than two or three boxes so occupied, in the same night. There is a notion in *England*, that the *Italians* frequently sup in their boxes, and that, by drawing the shutters in front, they may be in private; but there are no such shutters at *Naples*; and the practice of supping is so rare, that I have never seen it.

I am, Sir, &c.

LETTER XXI.

NAPLES, *Nov.* 1765.

SIR,

I Propose, in this letter, to give you a description of the great Opera-House; and as all the *Italian* theatres are built on the same plan, diff'ring only in the number of boxes, I desire you will consider it as a specimen of the others, tho' the Pit is indeed a little particular; for the seats have elbows, which circumstance, I believe, is peculiar to this one Theatre.

The Pit here, as I have already hinted, is very ample; it contains betwixt five and six hundred seats, with arms resembling a large elbow chair, besides an interval all through the middle, and a circuit all round it, under the boxes, both of which I judge, in a crowded house, will hold betwixt one and two hundred people standing. The seat of each chair lifts up like the lid of a box, and has a lock to fasten it. There are, in *Naples*, Gentlemen enough to hire by the year the first four rows next to the orchestra; who take the key of the chair home with them, when the Opera is finished, lifting up the feat, and leaving it locked. By this contrivance, they are always fure of the fame place, at whatever hour they pleafe to go to the Opera; nor do they difturb the audience, though it be in the middle of a fcene, as the intervals betwixt the rows are wide enough to admit a lufty man to walk to his chair, without obliging any body to rife. The ufual payment for the feafons, or the whole year, in which they give four operas, is twenty ducats, about three pounds fifteen fhillings; the people who do not hire their feats by the year, pay three carlines, about thirteen pence halfpenny, for their place in the pit.

The boxes are not difpofed like ours, into front and fide boxes, but into fix ranges, one above another, all round the houfe: The three lower ranges are hired either for the feafon, or the whole year, by the Ladies of diftinction: The price of a box for the whole year, is two hundred and forty ducats, equal to about forty-fix or forty-feven pounds fterling. The price of a feafon is proportioned to the length of the feafon: The other three ranges are let by the night; but no man or woman can go into the boxes, paying only for

for one person, as in *France* and *England*. Strangers who come to *Naples* for a short time, if they are either people of figure, or well recommended, are invited into the boxes of the nobility; if they are not, they hire a box for the night, and seldom fail to find one in the second or third range, for, should it happen that they are all taken up for the season by persons of quality, yet some of these persons of quality are not so delicate, but that they order the undertaker of the opera to let out their boxes when they do not go themselves, and often stay at home purposely on *gala* nights, and at the opening of a new opera, when, sometimes, they are hired for the night at an exorbitant price, such as fifteen ducats, and sometimes much more.

Each of the six ranges, consisting of thirty boxes, would make one hundred and eighty in all, if the King's box, in the front, did not occupy the place of four of them. It is situated on the same level with the second range, and is both of the extent and height of two boxes, possessing as I have intimated, the space of four boxes. This situation of his Majesty in front has a good effect, and if our Royal Family approved of it, the imitation would grace our *London* theatres.

The boxes are large enough to hold twelve people standing, but their largeness is owing to their depth, for they are so narrow, that only three Ladies can sit in front, and the three next behind them must stand up, if they would see all the stage and the actors; so that if more than six are present, all those behind see little or nothing: This arises from a partition which runs betwixt each of the boxes, and prevents the side view. Were these partitions removed, the house would be much cooler in warm weather; two or three hundred people more would partake of the diversion than there do at present; the Ladies would be more conspicuous, and, consequently, the theatre appear more gaudy than now that they are shut up in such dark closets; but I should suppose that this alteration will never take place, because if the boxes which now hold six only with convenience, were made commodious for ten or fifteen, two families would join for one box, and consequently, not above half the boxes would be hired. What I have here said, relates only to the side boxes, because every one in the front boxes must have a view of the stage.

I am, Sir, &c.

LETTER XXII.

NAPLES, *Dec.* 1765.

SIR,

IT is the custom in *Italy* to light the stage only, which renders their spectacles frightfully dark and melancholy. They pretend it is an advantage to the performers and the stage; and so far is true, that if there must be only such a small quantity of light in the house, it is much better to place it on the stage, than on any other part; but on *gala* nights, when it is illuminated in every part, the *Italians* seem as much pleased with it as a stranger, so that I imagine it is to save the expence of so many wax tapers, that the custom is continued. These tapers are almost as big as small torches, and are disposed very unartfully against the sides of the boxes, as high as the fourth range; so that the glare, the heat, and the smell of them, are very offensive to those who sit in the boxes, on which account, it is not unusual, on the *gala* nights, when the King is not there, to see the people in the boxes extinguish several of them. When his Majesty is present, they do not take

that

LETTER XXII.

that liberty; but if, inſtead of theſe tapers, there were a ſufficiency of luſtres hanging over the pit, the purpoſe would be anſwered without the leaſt annoyance.

Dark as the boxes are, they would be ſtill darker, if thoſe who ſit in them did not, at their own expence, put up a couple of candles, without which it would be impoſſible to read the opera; yet there are ſome ſo frugal, as not to light up their box, though the inſtances are rare. It is not the faſhion here, nor to the beſt of my remembrance, in any part of *Italy*, to take a ſmall wax-light to the houſe, and, therefore, hardly any man has eyes good enough to make uſe of a book in the pit.

The Ladies in the boxes and pit of the Opera Houſe in *London*, make a much more brilliant appearance than they would in the dark boxes at *Naples*, where, on common nights, it is not poſſible to diſtinguiſh a feature in the oppoſite boxes: Indeed the *London* theatres are much better contrived to render the ſpectators an ornament to the houſe; for even the galleries in my opinion, exhibit a proſpect which enlivens, if it do not beautify, the ſcene; but were they ever ſo aukward, they are neceſſary in *England*, where ſo many hun-

dreds

LETTER XXII.

dreds of the middle rank of people, resort every evening to the Play-house. The theatres at *Paris*, from their enormous length, are rather worse shapen than those of *Italy*; but their amphitheatre behind the pit, somewhat resembling our front boxes, is a great relief to them, otherwise, being so narrow, they would appear extremly melancholy. It is wonderful, that so gay, so elegant a nation should be satisfied such a length of time with two Tennis-courts converted into Play-houses; but I am apt to suspect from some conversations I have had with *Frenchmen* on this subject that the force of a long habit, has led them into an opinion, that theatres should be constructed in that form, and possibly were they to build two theatres for their *French* and *Italian* plays, they would adopt the same plan. Were an audience to consist of the fine people only, *Palladio*'s theatre at *Vicenza* would unquestionably be the proper model, where the plan is half an oval cut length ways, surrounded with boxes ranged in a colonade, and where all the seats rise above one another so artfully, as to make the spectators themselves a most pleasing part of the spectacle.

The

LETTER XXII.

The men in the pit do not, upon the whole, make a good figure; for though there are many officers, who are well dreſt, yet they and the Gentlemen are much the ſmaller portion of the company there. There is a vulgar ſet of men who frequent the pit, and another ſet ſtill more vulgar, who pay nothing for their entrance, ſuch as the upper ſervants of the Ladies who have boxes, the upper ſervants of ambaſſadors, and ſometimes, for a ſmall fee to the door-keepers, thoſe ſervants introduce their friends. It is not to be omitted, amongſt the objections to the immenſe largeneſs of the houſe and ſtage, that, in windy weather, you would imagine yourſelf in the ſtreets, the wind blows ſo hard both in the pit and boxes; and this ſeldom happens without cauſing colds and fevers.

The performers are not paid ſo liberally at *Naples* as at *London*, but conſidering the different expence of living in the two places, the proportion is not very ſhort amongſt the capital ſingers, as may be gathered from the ſalary of *La Gabrieli*, who received for ſinging the laſt year, eighteen hundred ſequins, (nine hundred pounds ſterling) and has contracted for the ſame ſum, the enſuing year. *Aprile,*
the

the first man, has three thousand five hundred ducats. *Genaro*, the first dancer amongst the men, has two thousand ducats, and *La Morelli*, the first woman dancer, one thousand five hundred ducats. A ducat is worth about three shillings and ten pence.

The impressario, or manager, is bound to very bad terms, so that his profits are inconsiderable, and sometimes he is a loser. The theatre being a part of the palace, the King reserves for himself, his Officers of State, and Train, fifteen boxes; nor does the King (or rather the Regency) pay the manager one farthing, whereas the late King used to present him annually four thousand ducats. The junto deputed by his Majesty to supervise the Opera, reserve to themselves the right of nominating singers and dancers, which obliges the manager sometimes to pay them an exorbitant price. Another disadvantage he lies under, is, the frequent delay of payment for the boxes, and a manager must not take the liberty to compel persons of quality to pay their just debts.

You will wonder how I became possessed of these particulars; accident threw them in my way, and you may depend on their authenticity.

LETTER XXII.

The two burletta Opera Houses are not in much request, except when they happen to procure some favourite composition, the grand Opera being the only object of the *Neapolitans*, which, indeed, has such pre-eminent encouragement, that the others are forbidden, by authority, to bring any dancers on their stage, without a special licence, lest they should divert the attention of the public from the King's Theatre. I must not omit a foolish singularity, in relation to the women dancers at *Naples*, that, in consequence of an order from court, in the late King's time, they all wear black drawers. I presume it was from some conceit on the subject of modesty, but it appears very odd and ridiculous. I shall not enter into any detail of the two houses; but their dresses, their scenery, and their actors, are much more despicable than one could possibly imagine.

I am, Sir, &c.

LETTER XXIII.

NAPLES, *Dec.* 1765.

SIR,

THE play-houfe is hardly better than a cellar, and is really very much known by that name, being ufually called the *Cantina* (cellar.) You defcend from the ftreet down ten fteps into the pit, which holds feventy or eighty people, when crouded, each of which pays a carline, that is, four-pence halfpenny, for his admittance. There is a gallery round the pit, which is formed by partitions into ten or twelve boxes. Thefe boxes holding four perfons conveniently, let for eight carlines. Under thefe difcouragements it will not be difficult to conceive, that the fcenes, the dreffes, the actors, and the decorations of the houfe muft be very indifferent: It will not, however, be fo eafy to imagine the vulgarity of the audience, which chiefly confifts of men in dirty caps and waftcoats, in the pit; for the boxes are generally empty. All the *Italian* Gentlemen and Ladies are very indelicate in the article of fpitting before them, never making ufe of a handkerchief, or seeking a corner for that purpose; but in the *Cantina* their nastiness is offensive to the last degree, not only spitting all about them, but also on every part of the wall, so that it is impossible to avoid soiling your cloaths. This habit is carried by some to such excess, that I cannot but ascribe the leanness of many *Neapolitans*, and the sallowness of their complexions, to the abundance of this evacuation.

The drama is so little cultivated in *Italy*, that I believe they seldom or never act Tragedy, at least I have never yet heard of such a representation, nor has it been my good fortune to see a comedy of more than three acts. The present state of the stage here, is what it always must have been in its infancy, before it became polished, and whilst the audience were a rude and illiberal people; that is to say, the principal entertainments seem to arise from double entendres and blunders, mistaking one word for another, and even from dirty actions, such as spitting or blowing the nose in each others faces; just as we see still practised in *England* by *Merry Andrews*, on the stages of Mountebanks, and on the outside of the booths in *Bartholomew-Fair*; but what
appears

LETTER XXIII. 97

appears moſt eſſential to the delight of a *Neapolitan* audience, are two or three characters, ſuch as *Punch* and the Doctor's man, who ſpeak the dialect of the lower people, which is unintelligible to a foreigner, however well he may underſtand pure *Italian*; and it is chiefly by theſe characters that the company is recreated, not only with the poet's obſcenities, but alſo as many looſe jokes of the actors as their extempore wit and humour can ſuggeſt. The rage for this ſpecies of comicalneſs is ſuch, that even in their burlattas they introduce one or two perſonages, who ſpeak *Neapolitan*, and I queſtion whether a ſerious opera would be borne without them, if the populace frequented that theatre.

Notwithſtanding the unfavourable light in which I have placed theſe actors, I really think the *Italians*, by nature, have a genius for comedy; and, were the audience of this playhouſe more elegant and more reſpectable, ſome of theſe very actors would appear to have great talents; but, at preſent, they ſtand ſo little in awe of criticiſm, that they do not ſtudy the leaſt decorum, and are even ſo negligent in learning their parts, that I have ſometimes heard them prompted every word,

G 3   in

in the same manner as the fingers are in the recitativo of an opera. Amongst the few actors of merit, there is one who always represents a character called *Don Fastidio*; this man is so very unaffected and natural in all he says and does upon the stage, that, with a little correction, he would make a great figure on the theatre of *London* or *Paris*.

It would conduce much to the improvement of the manners and literature of this people, were some of the Quality to give their protection to the stage. It cannot be doubted that a *Mæcenas* would now, as formerly, in the same climate, call forth the poetic spirit; and it is a little wonderful that this event does not take place, as there is a kind of propensity amongst them to perform Comedy; for, during the Carnival, there are three or four plays represented several nights, by private persons, and by Convents, at their own expence, which meet with great applause; and, amongst others, there is one given by the *Cælestine* Monks, which is extremely celebrated. They perform with remarkable humour and exactness, nor do the Fathers scruple to wear womens dresses, and appear in very lascivious characters.—How extremely capricious! that the same mother-church should suffer her sons to play at *Naples*, and deprive the poor *French* comedians of Christian burial for acting at *Paris*.

I am, Sir, &c.

LETTER XXIV.

NAPLES, *Dec.* 1765.

SIR,

THE populousness of *Naples* is so remarkable, that a stranger, the first time he passes through some parts of the city, would imagine the people were assembled in the streets on some extraordinary occasion; but the truth is, that thousands of the populace (called the *Lazaroni*, or Black-Guards) have no other habitation than the streets, and much the greater part of the other portion having no employment, either from the want of manufactures, or their natural disposition to idleness, are sauntering in the streets from morning to night, and make these crowds, which are not seen in other places, but upon festivals, elections, &c. It is computed that

LETTER XXIV.

Naples contains three hundred, or three hundred and fifty thousand inhabitants; some exaggerate the number to four hundred thousand, but if there are three hundred thousand, it is much more populous than either *London* or *Paris*, in proportion to its extent; and I suppose it is the only metropolis in *Europe* which furnishes its own inhabitants: All the others are supplied with people from the provinces, the luxury and expensiveness of large cities being so great an impediment to marriage and populousness, that they would all, in the ordinary course of nature, be depopulated in a few years, were they not annually recruited from other parts; but in *Naples* the case is different, from a singular custom amongst the gentry in hiring married, in preference to unmarried servants. In *Paris*, or *London*, very few servants can hope to be employed who are not single, and, therefore, a great number of this class of people pass their lives in celibacy, as the instances are but rare, in those cities, where footmen and maid-servants can support themselves after marriage by a different occupation.

In *Naples* it is almost an universal fashion to keep their men-servants at board-wages, not admitting them to sleep in their houses:

LETTER XXIV.

This naturally leads them into marriage, as it gives them a settlement so essential to the character required here by all ranks of masters; but what seems still more to facilitate matrimony, in this order of people, is, the prodigious number of young women ready to accept the first offer; for in *Italy* they are not taken into service, as in *England*. A Nobleman who keeps forty men-servants, has seldom more than two maids; and, indeed, it is so much the province of the men to do the house business, that they are employed all over the country, even to the making of the beds. This circumstance, with the difficulty a woman has to acquire her living here by any other means, is the reason why they seldom make an objection to the certain poverty attending matrimony. The swarms of children in all the streets, inhabited by the poor, are such as will necessarily result from this practice; and as a married couple, though they have six or seven children, never occupy more than one room, the extreme populousness of *Naples* must, consequently, follow from such causes.

I have not been able to procure an annual list of the births and burials at *Naples*, but am told that each parish Priest can give an exact account of those in their respective parishes; and, therefore, it should seem an easy matter to publish the sum total, if the government esteemed it an object worthy of their regard. I presume, however, should this publication ever take place, that the number of births will be found to exceed that of their burials very considerably.

The Lazaroni, or Black-Guards, are such miserable wretches as are not to be seen in any other town in *Europe*; perhaps amongst the ashes of our glass-houses in *London*, you may find two or three beggars not unlike them; but here the number is said to be six thousand, not one of which ever lies in a bed, but upon bulks, benches, &c. in the open streets; and, what is scandalous, they are suffered to sun themselves, a great part of the day, under the palace walls, where they lie basking like dirty swine, and are a much more nauseous spectacle. Being almost naked, they suffer extremely in cold weather, and were the climate less mild, they would certainly perish; even the greater part of the poor, who work for their livelihood, seldom wear shoes or stockings, and their children never; but, notwithstanding the power of use, the cold in the

winter

winter months produces chilblains and sore legs to a piteous degree. When the spring advances, they strip their infants entirely, and spare some little expence by that œconomy. The Convents at *Naples* are rich, and make a practice of distributing broth and bread, once a day, to those who apply for charity; and it is by this charity that the Lazaronis principally subsist, though by pilfering and begging, some of them acquire enough to satisfy the necessities of nature, and even to appear healthy and robust.

I am, Sir, &c.

LETTER. XXV.

NAPLES, *Dec.* 1765.

SIR,

TO give you an idea of the starving life of the major part of the poor, I shall only mention the wages of servants, to which all kinds of wages are nearly proportionable. A *Neapolitan* Gentleman pays his footman five ducats a month; a Nobleman, perhaps, six;

All

All the Quality who keep pages, give them six or seven ducats, with a livery once in two years, and another for *gala* days only, which lasts ten years; but neither shoes, stockings, nor washing: With this sum they subsist themselves and families, for their pay includes board-wages; nor are the tables of the Gentry so amply provided here as to admit of the least depredation, as is the case in *England*, where married servants generally maintain their wives from their master's larder. Now a ducat is about three shillings and nine-pence, five of which make something less than nineteen shillings, the whole monthly income of far the greater number of livery servants in *Naples*, as the fashion of vails is in a manner unknown, except by great chance, or at the beginning of the year, when they receive a few trifling perquisites. The generality of servants marrying very young, their wives are, for the most part, blest with a numerous progeny, the cares of which are a sufficient occupation for the wife, so that the labour of her hands can add but little to their stock. The rent of a room for a month, is a ducat, which leaves exactly fifteen shillings for cloathing and maintaining the whole family. After this detail,

it

it will not appear strange that they seldom have either meat or fresh fish, but find themselves under the necessity of feeding chiefly on the produce of gardens, a cheap sort of cheese, salt-fish, and a coarse bread, the last of which articles is unfortunately as dear or dearer at *Naples* than at *London*. I have conversed with *Neapolitan* Gentlemen, who seemed as much astonished as myself, at the possibility of bringing their expences within the compass of their wages; and yet if this be wonderful, how much more is it so to live on four ducats only, or four ducats and a half, which is the usual price given by the lawyers and trading people; for every body here has the rage of keeping a footman, down to a sett of housekeepers, who hire one for the *Sunday* only; and there are some who hire one for an hour or two only; so that there are servants who let themselves out to three or four different masters on the same *Sunday*, it suiting one master to have his servant in the morning, another at noon, and a third after dinner, &c. This class of servants are wittily called *Domenichini* by the *Neapolitans*, from an allusion to the word *Domenica*, signifying *Sunday*. I am not to forget, that in the great families a few

of

of the upper servants are not at board-wages, but are dieted by their masters, for the convenience of consuming what remains at table.

The King's footmen receive only eight ducats and six carlines a month, equal to 1*l*. 12*s*. 6*d*. and two carlines a day extraordinary, when his Majesty is at any of his palaces out of *Naples*. This extraordinary allowance is granted them for their particular maintenance, as they cannot partake of the same dinner with their wives and families.

I shall close this account of the lowness of servants wages, with remarking, that they all prefer a carline (four-pence halfpenny) a day for board-wages, to the being maintained by their masters; by which one may judge with what vile provision they can subsist. They know nothing of the superfluities so common amongst our poor; I mean the excessive use of strong and spirituous liquors, a matter of such notoriety, that I do not remember to have seen in the streets one drunken man or woman, if I may except a few soldiers, and a few *Valets-de-Place*. Indeed the custom or spirit of sobriety, is rooted so deeply in their manners, that the luxury they indulge, is a passion for snow or iced-water, and lemonade,

nade. You fee the very dregs of the mob fpending their farthing or halfpenny on a glafs of thofe liquors, in the coldeft feafon of the year; the fame thing is practifed by the great, in a more elegant and expenfive manner: Perhaps the heat of the climate may have indicated this luxury firft, in the fummer months; but it is now become one of the neceffaries of life, and the Government has availed itfelf of the fafhion, by making a monopoly of the fnow at *Naples*, and felling it at a very high price, about three farthings a pound. By the bye, the prejudices in favour of the wholefomnefs of fnow, or ice, and alfo their medicinal qualities, have prepoffeffed the phyficians here beyond all credibility. It is not to be imagined how fanguine they are in the relations they give of their miraculous effects in moft inflammatory diforders of the head, the lungs, and the bowels; and they not only in thefe cafes prefcribe them inwardly, but likewife apply them externally. It is almoft rude to doubt in converfation the virtue of this remedy, becaufe they produce a thoufand inftances of wonderful cures, wrought in their own practice; but we know the advocates for hot water have

like-

likewife, in the very fame cafes, pretended, from experience, the fame good effects; and, perhaps, were the truth known, Nature, in all the inftances, may have done more than either of the parties fufpect, and, poffibly have worked a cure, in fpite of their boafted medicines.

I am, Sir, &c.

LETTER XXVI.

NAPLES, *Dec.* 1765.

SIR,

WHAT I faid in my former letter with regard to the cheapnefs of fervants, will account for the fhewy appearance fome of the Quality make here, with fmall fortunes; but what enables them alfo to fupport a large houfhold, and a vaft quantity of coach horfes and carriages, is the circumftance of confining themfelves to that one luxury. They have no expenfive country-houfes and gardens, no hounds, no race-horfes, no parliament elections, and, in fhort, no great demands

LETTER XXVI.

mands for the education of their children, difpofing of all the girls in convents, upon very eafy terms, whilſt they are children, where they are left all their lives, unlefs they provide them hufbands; for ſingle young Ladies are not fuffered to appear in the world, neither at fpectacles nor vifits.

Another reafon why the *Neapolitan* Gentry can figure with their equipages, is, the very fmall expence they admit at their tables. It is not ufual here to dine or fup at each others houfes, and there are fome who never do, except only on *Chriſtmas-Day*, or, perhaps, during the week; nay, they are, in general, fo unaccuftomed to entertain one another, that the greater number feldom receive their friends but upon weddings, deaths, and lyings in: They alfo carry their parfimony fo far, as to lock up their fine furniture in the intervals of thofe ceremonies. Upon thefe occafions they are very pompous, and, what, is extraordinary, the lying-in Ladies receive company in great crowds, the day after their delivery, which, however, as foon as the compliments are paid, retire immediately into the adjacent chambers, where they form themfelves into card parties, or *converzationi*, and

H   are

are regaled with every dainty the confectioner can furnish: these compliments are continued nine days. It is also the fashion to visit the widow, or nearest relation of the deceased, the day after his or her death; and this compliment of condolance is likewise paid by every acquaintance, before the expiration of nine days.

It is amazing at how small a charge the generality of the first people live here, for their kitchen. It is not an uncommon thing to contract with the cook, or one of the upper servants, to supply their dinners, at so much a head, and I shall hardly be credited, when I mention so small a sum as nine-pence *English*, wine included; nevertheless it is a practice not only at *Naples*, but *Rome*, and other cities of *Italy*, and is a fact that may be depended on. However, it must be understood that there are a few exceptions amongst the Nobility to this retired manner of eating: There are some, who, when they entertain, give the most splendid, expensive, and elegant dinners that can be imagined. The Prince of *Franca Villa* keeps a kind of open table every night, with twelve or fourteen covers, where the *English* of any figure are at all times received

LETTER XXVI.

ceived with the greatest politeness. Though it be not the custom to dine or sup with one another, except on extraordinary occasions, their visits being mere conversations, yet, during the Carnival, some few exert themselves so far as to give balls, and even some of the merchants adopt this practice; but the Princess of *Franca Villa* this season gave three in one week, where the company amounted to seven or eight hundred people each time. Now I have mentioned visiting, it may be worth remarking, on a certain tiresome etiquette prevailing in this place, of waiting in the streets on evening visits, till two pages give in your name, and bring down flambeaux to light you up stairs, perhaps almost to the top of the house, as the Quality live, for the most part, a great height from the ground; but this ceremony is much more inconvenient at the Opera House, when you are invited to a box, as you sit in your coach, to the obstruction of all others, till one or two pages come down with their flambeaux to conduct you to your seat.

The general custom of spending so little in other articles of luxury, leaves them the means of indulging their passion for shew and equipages; accordingly, some of their Princes have forty or fifty coach-horses, more than twenty different carriages, thirty, forty, or fifty domesticks and pages, besides four or five (and I once saw six) running footmen before their chariots. A running footman seems almost an indispensible necessary of life here; for a Gentleman never rides post on the road near *Naples*, nor takes an airing, without being preceded by one of these poor breathless fellows. It may be observed, however, that a running footman in the crowded streets of *Naples* is very useful, where the pavement is so smooth, and the noise of the crowd so great, that the motion of a coach is hardly heard, and many would be trampled by the horses, if they had not timely notice to get out of the way.

This love of shew seems to be more the characteristick of an *Italian* than even of a *Frenchman*, and is a striking novelty to an *Englishman*. In *Great Britain*, when a Gentleman can live comfortably within doors, and has a surplus, he thinks of a coach; but in *Italy* a coach and servants seem to be the first object, and when they are provided, they do as they can for the rest. The *Italian* turn

for

for grandeur appears not only in this splendour of their equipages, but in the very genius of their language. What we call in *England* a little crash of musick, composed of two or three instruments, is pompously stiled in *Italy* an *Academia*: If you send your servant on a trifling halfpenny errand, he tells you, upon his return, he has executed the *ambasciata*; and so in other instances.

I am, dear Sir, &c.

LETTER XXVII.

Naples, *Dec.* 1765.

SIR,

THOUGH the Dukes and Princes here are said to have immense estates, nevertheless, excepting two or three, they are not to be compared to those of our *English* Nobility. The Prince of *Franca Villa*'s amounts, as I have been informed, to about thirteen thousand a year, and no Prince makes a greater figure at *Naples* than he.

The emoluments of the great officers of State, and the falaries of all the King's fervants, are much fmaller than in *England:* The fees alfo of lawyers and phyficians are trifling, compared with thofe in *England*; and talents of every kind are but poorly recompenfed, fo that affluence is not diffufed through every ftreet, as in *London*, but is confined almoft within the narrow circle of the Nobility: The following fpecimens will give you an idea of the fmallnefs of their court appointments:

The Lord Steward, Lord Chamberlain, and Mafter of the Horfe, have each eighteen hundred ducats a year, not three hundred and fifty pounds fterling; and about twenty-fix fhillings a day for their table, when the King is not at *Naples*. The Mafter of the Horfe has likewife a coach and fix, two running footmen, and two footmen at the King's expence. The Lords of the Bedchamber have but thirty ducats a month, which is about feventy pounds a-year, and thirteen fhillings a day for their table, when the King is at any of his country palaces; but there are no perquifites attached to thefe employments: It is therefore not to be wondered at, that fo

many

LETTER XXVII.

many of the Nobles with small estates, though they have a place at court, are obliged to live retired, notwithstanding the low price of eatables and labour.

It is probable, that, with good management, their estates would bring in a much larger income to them, and a more comfortable subsistence to their tenants. I have, in conversation with Gentlemen of fortune, intimated, that, would they parcel and lease out their estates in large farms, the farmer would improve the land, and enrich both the proprietor and himself; but they do not see so far, and grudge the tenant a better livelyhood than roots and brown bread. In consequence of this maxim of keeping down their tenants, their farms are so very small, that it seldom happens that the farmer pays his rent in cash; but the landlord receives it in kind; so that a Nobleman is obliged every year to sell corn, wine, oil, and silk, and employ a great number of stewards for that purpose, who are said to defraud them very grosly.

From this state of the case it should appear, that the value of the lands is not so great as it ought to be, and as it certainly will be, whenever they shall encourage agriculture, by suffering their tenants to acquire property, and the Government shall think proper to reform the police, in removing the heavy duties on the exports of this country, such as silk, corn, oil, &c. and lay them on the luxurious imports.

I am, Sir, &c.

LETTER XXVIII.

NAPLES, *Dec.* 1765.

SIR,

THERE does not seem to be much current coin in this kingdom, at least not much gold, so that every considerable payment must be made either in their bank-bills, or in silver; indeed there is so much larger a proportion of silver than gold, that an allowance of one third *per Cent.* (six shillings and eght-pence) is given in the exchange: This scarcity of gold is very inconvenient, and I have seen five or six Gentlemen sit down at cards, under the necessity of marking their losings, as none of them were provided
with

with gold; and four or five guineas in silver being too great a weight for the pocket, not one of them had money to any value about him. The *Neapolitans*, who, like all other people on the earth, are not a little diffatisfied with their adminiftration, afcribe the fcarcity of gold to a bad police, and to the exceffive duties on their exportations, which make the ballance of trade run fo heavily againft them; but notwithftanding there is fo much larger a proportion of filver than gold, the proportion of copper is ftill greater with refpect to the filver, infomuch, that the retail traders are overloaded with it to a degree that obliges them to make a certain allowance for the exchange; and in confequence of this neceffity, you fee in the market-places and ftreets, great numbers of money-changers, who have a little ftall, heaped with copper money, which they deliver out for filver to thofe who want change; and they receive of the fhop-keepers about a halfpenny for every four fhilling's worth; fo that if they difpofe of as much copper as produces one hundred fhillings, they earn that day one fhilling and a halfpenny. The carline (four-pence halfpenny) is worth ten grains. The grain (not quite a

half-

halfpenny) confifts of twelve calli (cavalli), and the leaft piece of coin is three of thefe calli, with which the poor can purchafe a fmall bit of cheefe, chefnuts, apples, and other fruits, on which they feem to fubfift, almoft as much as on bread.

About two years fince, there was a great fcarcity of bread in this kingdom, which produced very fatal effects. Frequent mention was made of it in our *London* news-papers, but I do not remember that our ideas anfwered to the horrors which really attended it. It began in *December* 1763, and was followed by a ficknefs. The famine and the ficknefs together, carried off, as they compute, betwixt three and four hundred thoufand people. There were fome villages almoft entirely depopulated, only two or three perfons furviving the fury of one or the other of thefe calamities. It is faid that near fifty thoufand were deftroyed in the city of *Naples* only. From the relations I have heard and read, it feems to me wonderful that it fhould have ceafed fo fuddenly as it did, fince, in fome of the cafes, it bore ftrong marks of a plague, the moft robuft dying in two or three days after being feized, befides that, bubos and carbuncles were no uncommon symptoms. The distress of the poor was so great, that they were glad to get the food of the very dogs, which now and then produced a spectacle shocking to human nature; for the famished animals were sometimes seen feeding on the dead bodies of such who died in the streets, the moment after they expired. A twopenny loaf not only sold at this time for fourteen-pence, a sum as much above the abilities of the poor as a guinea, but often it was not to be purchased; and it was no unusual thing, when friends dined upon an invitation at each others houses, to take their own bread with them. There was a charitable endeavour set on foot, to distribute bread, at a low price, amongst the poor. Some bakers, at a particular hour every day, delivered out, by his Majesty's command, and at his Majesty's expence, a certain number of loaves: but the design was entirely frustrated; for such only of the mob procured it who were stout, and could make their way with sticks, and other weapons, to the door. These people possessed themselves of all the bread at the low price ascertained by his Majesty, and sold it in the city at an enormous profit: In the mean while, the old, the sick,

and

and the decrepit, for whom, principally, this benevolent defign was calculated, as at the pool of *Bethefda*, could never partake of the bleffing. It is remarkable, that whilft the poor were groaning under this affliction, the moft abandoned fet of villains in the world, namely, the flaves aboard the galleys, and the prifoners in the feveral goals, by virtue of their ftated allowance of bread, enjoyed perfect health and happinefs.

I am, *Sir*, *&c.*

LETTER XXX.

NAPLES, *Dec.* 16, 1765.

SIR,

THERE are three days in the year, the 16th of *December*, the 4th of *May*, and, I think, the 19th of *September*, that the miracle of the liquefaction of St *Januarius*'s blood is performed in this city. I had the pleafure of going through the ceremony this morning at the Cathedral: One of the three times it is exhibited, not at the Cathedral, but in in the ſtreets, in a ſort of open portico, or pavilion, of which there are ſix in *Naples*, called Seggias, and theſe pavilions are honoured with the exhibition in turns. In the Cathedral, or St *Januarius*'s church, amongſt other chapels, there is one where the blood, or what is called the blood, is preſerved. It is contained in two different phials, one of which holds very near an ounce of the liquor, the other only a few drops. Both the phials very much reſemble the Ladies ſmelling-bottles for ſalts, the larger being a depreſſed ſpheroid; the ſmaller, a narrow cylindrical one: They are contained in a golden caſe, betwixt two circular glaſſes of about three inches diameter, ſupported on a thin pedeſtal, by which means when it is held up againſt the light, or a candle is placed behind, the ſpectator ſees clearly the bottles and their contents. Mr. *Addiſon* ſpeaking of this miracle, ſays, it is a bungling trick; but not entering into any explanation how it is done, or in what conſiſts the clumſineſs of the performance, we are left either to believe in, or ridicule the miracle, juſt as we are educated. For my part, I do not treat it as an impoſture which requires no dexterity nor ſcience; becauſe unbelieving Proteſtants

and

and scoffers have not very clearly demonstrated how the fraud is carried on. That it is a congealed substance (not unlike a lump of *Spanish* snuff) which melts either from the heat of the hand, the candles, or the atmosphere is probable, though it is equally probable that it may be of a nature to be liquified by some chymical fluid poured upon it a few minutes before it is exposed to the public. The operation of liquefying is generally executed in eight, ten, fifteen, or twenty minutes; to-day it was above an hour and a half; and as I find, by the thermometer, it was colder this morning than it has been any day during the whole winter, that circumstance might incline one to judge that the liquefaction is owing to the heat of the atmosphere. In *May* and *September* the season is much warmer and fitter for this operation, if it be effected by heat. Some Hereticks, finding how slowly the miracle operated, thought proper to retire, in order to save their bones; for the *Neapolitans* entertain an opinion that the Saint refuses to act when Hereticks are present; and as the refusal is esteemed ominous, they have sometimes chaced them very rudely from their altars. I overheard a woman

man declare that it muſt be owing to the preſence of ſome Proteſtants in the church, that the miracle went on ſo ſlowly. The *Scandalous Chronicle* ſays, that, once upon a time, the liquefaction not taking place, the people of *Naples* were ſo uneaſy, that the Government thought proper to give orders that the miracle ſhould never fail for the future, ſince which time it has never failed.

The liquefaction in the larger phial was very evident; in the ſmaller, the matter, after the miracle, appeared only of a more vivid red. I cannot ſay it reſembled blood very much in either of them. A philoſopher would not inſiſt on the liquefaction, to be convinced of a miracle; it would be enough for him (conſidering the periſhable nature of fluids) that the blood itſelf was preſerved without diminution fourteen or fifteen hundred years; but the believers do not ſee ſo far, and are in agonies till the *Te Deum* be ſung for its ſucceſs. You may eaſily conceive how eager the congregation is to kiſs ſo venerable a relick. I was one amongſt others ſo happy as to have it applied to my lips, to my forehead, and then to my breaſt, though the prieſt is in ſo great a hurry to bleſs the croud, that he

does

does not offer it to the generality on their breasts, but only to the lips, and perhaps the forehead. I shall not describe the other ceremonies of this grand day; the processions, the exhibition of all their images on the great altar, and the Mass, which is usually celebrated by the Archbishop, but was not to-day. I am not to tell you that St *Januarius* is the patron of *Naples*, their guardian Saint. There is a famous statue of him at *Pozzoli*, a few miles off, which the *Saracens*, in one of their expeditions to this kingdom, wantonly defaced, by breaking off his nose, and putting it in their pockets; upon which, storms arose, and continued blowing so violently, that they could never put to sea, till, providentially, some of them thought it was owing to the resentment of the image, who would not be appeased so long as his nose was in their possession; upon which they threw it into the sea; and fine weather immediately succeeding, they sailed prosperously to their havens. In the mean while, the artists endeavoured to repair the image with a new nose, but neither art nor force could fasten one on; at length, some fishermen took up the original nose in their nets, but disregarding it, because they
did

did not know what it was, they flung it again into the sea; neverthelefs, the nofe continuing to offer itfelf to their nets, in whatever place they fifhed, they began to conceive it muft be fomething fupernatural; and one, more cunning than the others, fuggefted it might be the nofe of the Saint, upon which they applied it to the ftatue, to examine whether it fitted, and immediately, without any cement, it united fo exactly, as hardly to leave any appearance of a fcar; in which ftate we fee it. I do not infift upon your believing all the particulars of this miracle; but, let me tell you, I have feen fome thoufands to-day, who would think you a vile wretch if you do not.

I hope the above defcription will give you an idea of the machine which contains the two phials of blood; if it do not, you are only to conceive a very flat watch, of three inches diameter, without a dial-plate, &c. and with glaffes both before and behind it, in which cafe you would fee the movement of the watch, as you now do the phials: By this method of inclofing the phials, the heat of the hands can have very little effect on them, fo as to liquefy their contents.

LETTER XXIX.

We live in a quarter of the town called St *Lucia*, a Saint, as the Legend informs us, who, in the perfecution of the Chriftians, under *Dicclefian*, had her eyes torn out by the executioner; which circumftance has given her a great reputation for working miracles on every fpecies of blindnefs. Her chapel is clofe to our houfe, and the day before yefterday was her anniverfary. I attended the fervice both morning and afternoon, to fee the method of cure. In the midft of the chapel is a paltry wooden image of her faintfhip, with a platter in her hand, containing the reprefentation of two eyes. All the patients pafs their hands over thefe eyes, and immediately rub their own, before the virtue exhales. There is a fmall piece of bone fet in filver (a filver arm) which they pretend to be a relick of the faint; this they kifs, which likewife operates miraculoufly; but I obferved, moft of the patients take the advantage of both methods. At the church door there are feveral ftalls, where they fell prints of the martyr; the very pooreft of the difeafed can afford to buy the cheapeft: I was offered one for fo fmall a fum as three calli, which is not quite half a farthing.

It

LETTER XXIX.

It is said to have been a practice amongst the Heathens, not only to upbraid, but even to chastise their Gods, when they were not propitious to their prayers; the same thing is said of the lower class of people amongst the *Neapolitans:* If a *Madona*, or any particular Saint upon whom they depend, do not answer their expectation, they will sometimes behave very rudely on the occcasion. I cannot say I have seen any instance of this grossness; but, surely, if ever a Saint deserved punishment, it is the same *Santa Lucia*. Had you beholden the prodigious number of blind people I did that day in the neighbouring streets, who have come from year to year for her succour, I do not doubt but you would have cudgelled her like the *Medecin malgré lui*, into the exertion of her powers; I mean, upon the supofition that you were one of this sort of Catholicks.

I am, Sir, &c.

LETTER XXX.

NAPLES *Jan.* 1766.

SIR,

IT must be in consequence of the precariousness of punishment, that this city furnishes many more delinquents, in proportion to its dimensions, than our wicked *London*. I think there are in the prisons here, about four or five thousand, (suppose two or three thousand) besides about two thousand in the galleys, lying in the harbour. Those in the galleys are chained two and two, and may be thought to suffer from lying on the decks; but their condition is far preferable to that of many of the poor, who lie in the streets; besides, that they have a certain allowance of bread from the King, and even some cloathing; but above all, and what renders the life of a poor *Neapolitan* happy, they are, in a manner, exempt from labour; for very few are employed in cruizing, or other business: What work they do aboard the vessels, is chiefly for their own benefit, and, I may say, luxury. If a taylor, a shoe-maker, or any other handicraftsman earns a few pence, he puts a part of it

at

at least into his pocket, and purchases some rarity, the government, as I have intimated before, furnishing him with bread. The galleys lye very near my lodgings, and I have often diverted myself with speculating on the lives and manners of these slaves. The *Neapolitans* are not a gay mercurial people, but those aboard the galleys are by no means graver than those out of the galleys; and a man who has visited them so frequently as I have done, will never afterwards, when he means to picture extreme misery, represent it as the proverb does, in the shape of a galley-slave. I have seen a musician aboard, entertaining them with vocal and instrumental musick, whom I supposed one of their gang, but, upon enquiry, found he was a poor man, they paid for his performances when they were disposed to be merry; and I do not doubt but this poor man styled those we call wretches, his good masters. If then so sober, so phlegmatic a nation as *Italy*, find such delights aboard a galley, what do you think of the lively skipping *Frenchmen* in the galleys at *Marseilles?* I should suppose, take one with another, they are a jollier, happier set of people than our city *plumbs*. There are many
services

services, however, to which these idle fellows might be very properly destined, such as mending the horrid roads of this kingdom, which could not fail to redound to the honour and profits of the nation, and at a very small immediate expence; but, as I told you before, the police here is not on a good footing.

I have, in some of my letters, mentioned how often murderers escape unpunished, and have assigned it as the obvious reason, why murders are so much more frequent in *Naples* than *London*. Would you believe it possible, that a magistrate of this city, a few days since, declared to a Gentleman who interrogated him on this subject, that the preceding week the populace had been very orderly, for that only four murders had been committed! I have this account from very good authority, a *Neapolitan*, of great birth, and a high station, who attests it to be a fact. Perhaps, however prone the populous are to so atrocious a deed as murder, the relation may be exaggerated; yet certainly, they do not here hold it in such horror as we do in the colder climates. A young Gentleman informs me, that, on the road to this place from *Rome*, he saw, at a distance, a scuffle amongst some postilions,

in

in which, as it proved afterwards, one of them was ſtabbed dead. Upon an enquiry into the occaſion of the tumult, his meſſenger was cooly anſwered, that it was a *colpo di coltello* (a ſtab with a knife.) If the guilty eſcape, or the innocent are convicted, you, an *Engliſhman*, will not admire at it, when I tell you that the plaintiff and defendant do not appear face to face before the judges, nor are the evidences confronted; but the method of trying criminal cauſes here, is, by the intervention of two *Scrivanos* (Attorneys) one on the ſide of the proſecutor, and the other of the delinquent, the firſt of which, ſtates the accuſation, and the other the defence; after that, the judges, by a plurality of voices, determine according to the nature of the evidence; a very looſe vague manner of deciding cauſes of this nature, and which muſt leave a door open to a thouſand ſubterfuges, chicaneries, and villanies; in fact, by this means juſtice is often eluded, either abſolutely, or for a length of time; and the delays of criminal cauſes become as tedious as the delays of civil cauſes.

It a little hurts me, that ſo many of my accounts from this kingdom ſhould ſeem ſevere. I deſire, therefore, you will remark, that my censures regard chiefly the morals of the lower people, and the gallantry of the great. I wish I could always write panegyric; for, speaking as an *Englishman*, every partiality allowable should be admitted in their favour. I assure you, the politeness of the *Italians* towards our nation, is very extraordinary: Towards the *French* they are not so cordial; that people, by their frequent and wanton invasions of *Italy*, for some few centuries past, have given birth to a national animosity, which will not soon be appeased.

There are not, as I have said, many of the Nobility who keep any kind of open table; but those who do, never fail to invite such *English* whose quality, connections, or recommendatory letters, render them proper company for people of the first rank. The Prince of *Franca Villa* closed the carnival last week with a splendid dinner, (perhaps more splendid than any you see in *London*,) provided for eighteen guests, ten of which were the *English* Gentlemen on their travels. I do not find, by my observations, that foreigners think so abjectly of us as we do ourselves. It is much for our honour that they do not read our news-papers, so filled with

groans,

groans, complaints, and despair, on the subject of our present state; for abroad we are esteemed a happy, rich, triumphant nation. Madam ————, a *German* Lady of the first distinction, has lately procured the good opinion of the *English*, by a *repartee*, which, however, came better from her mouth than it does from my pen, as it owes some part of its beauty to the emphasis with which she uttered it. It seems she had fallen into a slight altercation with a *Frenchman* on national subjects, and being a little provoked by his manner, which she thought vain and overbearing, she told him with some indignation, *Sir, you Frenchmen, I know, despise every nation under the sun, except the* English, *and them you hate; but you would despise them if you could.*

I am, Sir, &c.

LETTER XXXI.

NAPLES, *Jan.* 1766.

SIR,

YOU have no idea of the populousness of this city: Many of the streets resemble a crowded market; and, it is true, these streets are a kind of market; for the principal trade carried on here is for eatables. The street of *Toledo*, by far the most magnificent one in *Naples*, is very much disfigured by numberless stalls of this kind, which attract an infinity of customers; but I suppose another reason why *Naples* appears so much peopled, is, that very few manufactures are carried on there; and the lower class of people chusing rather to live on the charity of monasteries, than do any kind of work, are therefore always loitering in the streets; whereas our labouring artificers in *London* are generally shut up the whole day, either in shops, cellars, or garrets; but, upon the whole, I can venture to declare, that the streets in *London* appear like a desart, compared with many in *Naples*; which last almost resemble *King-street*, near *Guildhall*, when some popular or muti-

mutinous election is going forward. But if I wonder at the fullness of their streets, how shall I describe their *Vicaria*, their *Westminster-Hall*? If I remember well, Mr *Addison* says, that when a *Neapolitan* does not know what to do with himself, he tumbles over his papers in order to start a law-suit: But, sincerely, if the kingdom of *Naples* were as extensive as the Commonwealth of *Rome*, when at its highest pitch of glory, and every cause were to be tried in the capital, the thousands of lawyers you see here would answer to that idea; but how they are supported is to me a problem. The first time I went to the *Vicaria*, I was mortified to have set out so late from home, finding the streets crouded with advocates in their way to dinner; but notwithstanding the difficulty of threading the multitude, who were pouring out in such numbers, I found, when I had pushed into the hall, almost as much pressing as we usually meet with the first night of a new play in our *London* theatres. What a blessed country, where all who are not princes or beggars, are lawyers or priests!

I am, Sir, &c.

LETTER XXXII.

NAPLES, *Jan.* 1766.

SIR,

THE manner of burying their dead in *Italy* is at first very shocking to an *Englishman*. Their custom is, to carry the corpse, drest in his usual wearing apparel, with his face exposed, on an open bier, through the streets, to the church where the service is read,; after which it is stripped, and at a convenient hour, buried; but there is a pride and rivalship among the middling rank of people, in dressing out their dead children for this exhibition, which is truly laughable. The other day there passed under our window, the body of a boy, about eight years old, whose figure and face, were as hideous as death and the small pox could make them: Would you believe, the parents had dressed him in a fine laced hat, bag wig, blue and silver cloaths, &c. and, above all things, had not forgot to stick a sword on? I do not in the least doubt but the friends found a real consolation in the prettiness and richness of the corpse, and were amongst their neighbours

LETTER XXXII.

more occupied with this idea, than with that of the eternal absence of the child.—I have not had the good fortune to meet with an *Italian* yet, who is well enough read in the history and customs of his country, to inform me of the origin of this practice; but I should conjecture, that it was at first designed to prevent foul play. The reality of every man's death is now evident to the whole parish; and no young spendthrift can spirit away a father, or rich uncle, fill a coffin with stones, send it to the grave, and then take possession of the estate. I suppose some such imaginary evil, was the ground of this conceit; but it is a fashion I much condemn; for the aspect of death should never be suffered to become familiar to a people, with so much brimstone in their veins as the *Neapolitan* mob have. It were to be wished, that a dead, or dying man, were always a frightful object, and that the Police would study every art to terrify murderers; but there are ways to render men capable of butchering a man and a hog with the same indifference, and one would think, that at *Naples*, the magistracy had cultivated this art; for the most atrocious parricides, are seldom punished here. I think the last four years have furnished but four examples of executions; and, as if a fatality were to attend all their judgments, two of the four proved afterwards to have been innocent. If a murderer touch a church wall (and many walls are a church wall in this city) before he is seized by the officers, holy church will not admit him to be hanged.—Then take with you, that if one man stab another in the sight of ten witnesses, they all decamp, and leave the coast clear to the assassin, because the murderer and all the spectators, who remain with the corpse, are indiscriminately carried to prison; and justice for many days, and sometimes weeks, does not enquire, or at least distinguish, which is the criminal, and which are the witnesses. You will not therefore wonder at the difficulty of procuring evidence upon these occasions. Mr. *Hamilton*, the minister, gave up this year thirty two, who had taken sanctuary within the privileges of his walls, amongst which there were five or six murderers, and they all found means to be discharged the next day. There was a soldier executed last week, who complained that he was dealt very hardly with; and indeed it seemed rather an act of wantonness

LETTER XXXII.

ness in the executive power, than useful justice; for the poor devil had been in prison near six years, since his condemnation, and both he and his crime were forgotten long ago. For what reason he was produced to terrify murderers, I do not know; but I think a recent example, would have made more impression on this barbarous populace. He was a hardened dog, it seems, and availed himself of a ridiculous Gothick privilege, granted to criminals here, of having a sumptuous dinner before the execution, and inviting what friends he pleased to it.

I shall now give you a description of the Cocagna, a strange, wild, and barbarous entertainment given to the populace here four *Sundays* successively in the Carnival. Opposite to the King's palace, at thirty or forty yards distance, they build a kind of booth, with deal boards, of about the size of the largest booth in *Bartholomew* fair, but a little different in form, being rather a scaffolding than booth, and having no top or covering; there is some kind of order or architecture in it, there being at each end two large doors, supported each by two columns: You ascend by these doors into the body of the building, which

which rifes to a height equal to that of a moderate houfe in *London*. Upon the feveral parts of the fcaffolding, are intermixed a variety of bufhes and branches of evergreens; and behind the whole, and indeed in the midft of it, are fome painted fcenes, to render the object gaudy, and to deceive the eye with a view of a diftant landfcape. The fides of the building are ftudded with a prodigious number of loaves, placed in an architectical order, and likewife with a great quantity of joints of meat. Amongft the bufhes are thirty or forty living fheep, fome hogs, a few fmall beeves, and a great many living fowls. Now, the bufinefs of the day is to facrifice thefe poor creatures to the hunger of the mob; to do which with fome order, the foldiery, to the number of three thoufand men, furround the building, to keep off the people till the king appears in the gallery, who waves his handkerchief for a fign when to begin the ceremony. Upon this the foldiers open their ranks, and all the mob rufh in, and each, as he can, feizes his prey, and carries off the provifion and the living animals. The whole operation is almoft inftantly over. You may imagine they form into

little

LETTER XXXII.

little confederacies, or partnerships, for the more convenient execution of this purpose, and the carrying off a sheep or an ox. There has been in these riots much mischief done formerly, but this year I do not find that any man was either killed or hurt. The four companies of butchers, bakers, fishmongers, and poulterers, defray the charges of the four days. I cannot meet with any *Neapolitan* who knows the origin of this custom, or can tell me whether it be derived from the *Moors*, when they were in possession of some part of the *Sicilies*, or whether it be of Christian growth; or lastly, whether it be the remain, as is most probable, of some of the shews of wild beasts exhibited by the antient *Romans*, it answering exactly to the *Venatio Direptionis*.

An *Englishman* beholds with astonishment so many thousands collected together, and behaving so peaceably. In *London*, upon such an occasion of jollity and riot, one half of the croud would have been drunk; we should have seen one party quarrelling, another fighting, some laughing, all noisy; and, to compleat the confusion, perhaps, two or three dead cats hurled about from one to another, during the whole time of waiting. It appears,

pears to me, therefore, that, diabolical as the *Neapolitan* lower people are in their nature, when exasperated, they are much more under the restraint of order, when in good humour, than our mob.

I am, Sir, &c.

LETTER XXXIII.

NAPLES, *January* 1766.

SIR,

I BELIEVE I have writ you word, that in so large a city as *Rome*, there is not one hackney coach; an argument how few people can afford to ride, who do not ride in their own carriages. At *Naples* there is no other convenience of this kind than small chairs, such as we call sulkies, which, however, two people make a shift to sit in; they are drawn by a small horse, which scampers at a good rate, and the owner who lets it, stands behind, like a footman, with the whip, whilst the riders in the chaise hold the reins. The pavement of this city is amazingly good

and

and smooth, so that the draught is exceedingly small. It is a stone, composed of the materials within the bowels of Mount *Vesuvius*, which, when it burns, are liquefied into a mass, and, by the eruption, are poured down the mountain, into the circumjacent country. This liquefied matter, when it cools, becomes wonderfully hard, and makes the best pavement in the world; and it is thought by some antiquarians, that the famous *Roman* road, called the *Appian Way*, part of which has subsisted near two thousand years, was paved with the same stone, or rather lava, the proper name for this liquefied substance. You may imagine the fare of these sulkies is not great; they carry a man, at least a *Neapolitan*, for four-pence halfpenny, about a mile, and, if you keep them in waiting, it is about four-pence halfpenny an hour; but there is no fixed price, and a stranger should make a bargain. I have never yet rid out an airing in them, nevertheless, *Englishmen* of the first fashion take them for their excursions into the neighbouring towns and villages. They are likewise useful, as being expeditious; for all the job-horses in the coaches you hire, are such poor starved things, they can hardly drag you a moderate trot; and so wretchedly is this city provided with the luxuries, and indeed, many of the conveniences of life, that I question whether, if another foreigner were to come hither, he could possibly procure a coach, and a pair of job-horses; or, in other words, whatever engagements a foreign family may have made for the evening, if their horses were to be taken ill, they must stay at home, for the reason I have just assigned.

Surprising as this fact must appear to you, you will think it still more surprising, that in a metropolis said to contain three hundred and fifty thousand inhabitants, it should be difficult to find lodgings fit to receive a Gentleman; yet so it is; and there are few apartments to let here, equal in accommodation to what may be taken amongst the poor housekeepers in *Shoreditch:* But how can this possibly be the case, have I often cried out, when there are no courts of judicature in the kingdom, except those of *Naples,* where all the world must come to try their causes? I am answered, that is very true; but *Neapolitans* of every kind, from the highest to the lowest, satisfy themselves with these

accom-

accommodations: In short, except the house where I am, and another just by it, there are only two indifferent houses of reception in all *Naples*, whither strangers resort.

I write miscellaneously, as my thoughts occur; for, upon casting an eye over the preceding paragraphs of my letter, I perceive that I should have told you why the pavement in *Naples* is always so good; the reason is, that no heavy carriages ever pass over it; the heaviest are coaches, chariots, and wine carts; as most of the goods brought into, and carried out of the city, are upon a single ass's back. The gardeners, who are the paincipal traffickers, send their commodities on an ass, which returns laden with dung. I believe they are very impolitic in this particular, as a gardener who sends three asses loaden in this manner, might, with a small cart, send by those three asses, three times as much burthen, and return three times as much dung.

I am, Sir, &c.

LETTER XXXIV.

Naples, *March* 3, 1766.

SIR,

THE excursions from *Naples* are delightful; we are now making our country visits to all the neighbouring districts, where either nature or antiquity invites us. Upon the borders of our Bay, ran that range of beautiful villages and villas which were the residence and luxurious retirement of the *Romans*, in the times of their politeness and glory. Read *Horace* or some of Mr. *Pope*'s Imitations of *Horace*'s Satires and Epistles, and, if I remember rightly, you will meet with allusions to those places, and almost conceive of them as well as we ourselves do; for we only see the ground where those magnificent palaces and villas stood. Many of the noble *Romans* chose the circuit of this Bay for their country houses, and winter retreat. *Cicero* had one of his eighteen villas here. A great part of this coast lies exposed to the South sun, and under the brow of a cliff, which renders the climate here much hotter than that of *Naples*, so that though it be only

LETTER XXXIV.

only from five to ten miles distance, the fruits and herbage are a fortnight forwarder, than near the city.

At a town called *Puzzoli*, about half way to *Baia*, on one side of the Bay, they have within these few years discovered an antient temple, dedicated to *Serapis*, with some magnificent remains; and, amongst others, three pillars, of an immense diameter. Were *Martinus Scriblerus* here, he would be miserable to behold the little veneration shewn to these curiosities. I really believe, a Gentleman, with five thousand pounds a year, in *England*, would mortgage a part of it, to preserve the building in its exact form, with all the ornaments, paintings, &c. Here the King, or, rather, the regency, lays violent hands on the statues, pictures, &c. as they occur in digging, and transports them to some of the royal palaces, where they lose half their merit. Some of the paintings on the walls suffer extremely on the removal, and would be a precious relick, if properly preserved in their own places.

On the other side of the Bay is a city under ground, called *Pompeio*; it is about twelve miles from *Naples*. The short history of this

this town, is, that it suffered from an earthquake, and, amongst other buildings, a certain temple dedicated to *Isis*, was swallowed up. This temple was rebuilt, as appears from some inscriptions lately found, together with the temple itself; for the town being situated but a few miles from the neighbourhood of Mount *Vesuvius*, an eruption afterwards (I think in *Vespasian*'s time) from some one of these infernal caverns, threw up a sufficient quantity of dirt to bury the whole town, which has lain concealed from that time till within the last fifteen years, when a peasant, who was plowing or digging the ground, hit by chance against some stone, which, upon examination, led on to the above-mentioned temple of *Isis*. They are now removing the rubbish, by slow degrees, and have already made discoveries which interest every spectator who has the least curiosity. Besides the Temple, they have found the two gates of the High-Street, at about a mile's distance from each other, leading to *Naples*. The pavement is in as perfect order, as if the stones had been laid but yesterday, and the foot-path on each side is just like ours made lately in *Westminster*, though not quite so high.

LETTER XXXIV.

high. There are the bones of six or seven persons which lay in the prison when the eruption happened; from whence it may be concluded the town was not overwhelmed so suddenly, but that all the inhabitants, except these poor confined wretches, had time to escape.

Perhaps, could we know what a dreadful hollow we tread upon, and what a quantity of combustible matter there is within it, we should rejoice that we are on the point of leaving such treacherous ground: At present we comfort ourselves, that what happens only once in a thousand years, will hardly happen during our stay; but it really is curious, if not frightful, that, in a certain place called *Solfatarra*, not half a mile from *Puzzoli*, which abounds so with sulphur as to be almost intollerable to the nostrils, you not only hear the water boil under your feet like a great boiling cauldron, and in several places behold the hot steams issuing from below, but if you strike the ground with a rammer, or let fall a heavy stone, you are as sensible of a cavity underneath, as that a drum is hollow, from the sound it yields. In all this neighbourhood you have continually before your eyes a very

extra-

extraordinary phænomenon, a mountain called *Monte Nuovo* (the New Mountain) because it appeared suddenly in the night of the 29th of *September* 1538. That night there was a terrible earthquake in this place, which made great havock, and in exchange, the earth poured out from its bowels this monstrous mountain, which occupies the place, where, before that accident, there was even ground.

Miseno, so celebrated by the Antients, near which the *Roman* navy was usually stationed, cannot escape a traveller's regard when he is in its neighbourhood; but this promontory draws our particular attention from the manner in which *Virgil* speaks of it. It was very singular that he should characterise any place, by prophecying it would always bear the same name, but thus far his prophecy holds true; for, through a series of barbarous ages, it has preserved, and still does preserve the same name,.

——— *qui nunc Misenus ab illo*
Dicitur, æternumque tenet per secula nomen.

Herculaneum is the subterraneous town, whose name and reputation we are most acquainted with; but at present there is hardly any thing to be seen there; for, in proportion as they have emptied, they have filled it up up with dirt; and now, when you go under ground, you see nothing but a few remains of a theatre. The opening into it resembles, very much, the entrance into a large wine-vault. The antiquities found there are carried to the King's Palace at *Portici*, and compose a most curious Musæum. I shall not give you a list of the antient implements recovered from this city, but, amongst others, they have preserved the utensils of a *Roman* kitchen, such as a gridiron, spits, pots, *&c.* like those in modern use. There is a great collection of manuscripts, but, though they retain the form of an antique volume, upon handling, they prove tinder, and fall into a powder. They have a most ingenious device for separating one leaf from another, but the rottenness of the paper baffles their purpose, and it so seldom happens that they can detach an entire paragraph (which, by the bye, when it succeeds, is of little use) that they have given up all hopes of gratifying the world with the publication of these manuscripts. The learned have, probably, a great loss in this disappointment; they had flattered themselves, that the remaining books of *Livy*, and other valuable writings, might have been

found

found in this collection; now it is to be feared, that, though they should be there, we shall not avail ourselves of the possession.

The men who are removing the rubbish at *Pompeio*, are day-labourers, but the people first employed were the galley-slaves, who proved such cursed thieves, that they were obliged to dismiss them very soon; for no punishment, howsoever severe, deterred them from stealing every valuable antiquity that offered in their way; so impossible is it for fingers accustomed to pilfering, to refrain from the practice, when opportunity invites.

It may be remarked, that the common people of *Naples* are much addicted to larceny. An eminent merchant of this city tells me, that when he returns from his country-house, to town, for the winter, he constantly brings the window-casements home with him, and that every body who does not leave a servant, takes that method; for they would certainly be stolen if they were left. You will conceive, from this story, that country houses must be very paltry in this place, where they leave them open, and consequently without furniture all the winter.

The

LETTER XXXIV.

The gentry of this city have so few pursuits, that they are quite at leisure to follow any favourite study; and what seems to engage their principal attention, is, the means of preserving and lengthening life. This conceit is uppermost in their thoughts from morning to evening, and leads them into much quackery, and consequently into some whimsical opinions and practices. As I live close to the water-side, I see great numbers who come there to take a dose of health: They have a notion that the air which is blown from off the sea, is more wholesome than the air at land: They do not ride about, but sit still, and snuff it up, as a man takes rappee. Their notions in regard to a consumption, are dreadfully inconvenient to society; they are so fully persuaded of the contagiousness of this distemper, that when any of the family labour under it, they abandon them almost as cruelly as if they had the plague. Brothers and sisters are forbidden visiting each other, when any one of them is in this predicament; and it is a rule, without exception, to burn the doors, the hangings, and almost the whole furniture of a room in which any one dies of a consumption; and,

lately,

lately, they have begun the practice of removing the floor, for farther security. At first I smiled at this prejudice, but I soon found it offensive, not only to *Neapolitans*, but also to the *English* who have lived here some time. At present I hold my tongue when they talk on this subject. Men must not be contradicted in opinions which they esteem grounded on experience and matters of fact; more particularly when they think the facts have fallen within their own knowledge.

The whole navy of the kingdom of *Naples* is generally to be seen in this port; for, insignificant, as it may appear to an *Englishman*, it is much larger than they have any use for; and therefore it lies rotting in the docks and mole of *Naples*. The only purpose for which they employ their ships of war and frigates, is a cruise against the *Barbary* rovers; and this happens but rarely. They seem at length to have discovered, that gallies are but a poor defence against frigates, or even such vessels as our small privateers; for which reason, they never fit them out for sea, but reserve them merely for prisons. The following is a true list of the fleet: Two men of war; one of sixty-four guns, the other of fifty-four.

Two

LETTER XXXIV.

Two frigates of thirty-two guns each. Four gallies. Four galliots. Six xebecks.——A formidable navy against *Lilliput*, or their neighbouring potentate the Pope, should he declare war against *Naples*.

I am, Sir, &c.

LETTER. XXXV.

NAPLES, *March.* 1766.

SIR,

I HAVE not yet told you, that I saw the King's eldest brother a few weeks since: He is rarely visible, but the Regency think proper to exhibit him a few times in the year, namely, when the King removes from *Naples* to *Portici*, and from *Portici* to *Naples*. I took the opportunity, when the family came to town of entertaining myself with that spectacle. I met them half way on the road, and stood in a place where the coaches must necessarily pass near me. The administration act wisely in exposing him now and then, in this manner, to the eye of the public, as the very sight of him is a full vindication of their
conduct

conduct, in regard to the sentence of idiotism and disinheritance, passed on him some years since. The court was in mourning, but he was as well dressed as a youth in mourning can be, and his hair as well combed, and as well powdered. With all these advantages, however, the very first glance of him convinced me that he wants every one faculty of the mind. He has that wandering roll of the eye, which is peculiar to idiots and new-born infants; who, not having the endowment of thought and reflection, consequently cannot fix their attention to one object. There are some knavish quacks, and some silly doctors, who say, the cure is not impossible, and that he may be restored to his senses, which, by the bye, he never enjoyed in the least degree, from the hour of his birth. The opinion, however, might, in future times, be attended with pernicious consequences: A faction, in opposition to the King, his younger brother, might possess themselves of his person; affirm he had, by the virtue of some remedy, recovered his understanding, and attempt to place him on the throne. Perhaps I am too deep-sighted a politician, in looking so far into futurity; and, when I applaud the councils of *Spain*, for keeping

keeping him at *Naples*, in order to obviate such a mischief, perhaps they have no other meaning in it than avoiding the expence, the trouble, and the many inconveniences of a change of houshold, and of so long a journey, as that from *Naples* to *Madrid*. By what I can learn, he leads a happy kind of animal life. He eats and drinks with much pleasure, is subject to no gust of passion, and enjoys such infantine amusements, as a child in arms may be supposed to enjoy. Certainly the deprivation of reason is one of the greatest evils that can befall a man; and yet, possibly, whilst we are lamenting this Prince's destiny, that, by the loss of reason, he loses also his titles, his splendour, and his prospect of a throne; were he, as by right of birth he should be, Prince of *Asturias*, he might then be cursed with ambition, disappointment, and impatience for a crown, so as to render him a more miserable being than he now is.

The equipages which attended his Majesty and the court, were mean, old, and paltry, to a degree truly curious; therefore, if ever you hear the King of *Naples*'s fine coaches mentioned, you must understand it of those he uses only on *gala* days, and not of those he travels in. The coaches of *Naples* are not so magnificent as those of *Rome*, but are more numerous in proportion to its size, than in any city of *Europe*. At *Rome*, some of the coaches are very splendid, but they want the taste with which the *Paris* coaches are both built and painted; besides, that the *Paris* varnish gives them an unspeakable beauty. I am delighted with the liveries at *Rome*, which I think are sumptuous and not tawdry. The lace of them is neither gold nor silver, but silk and worsted, extremely rich, and about two inches and a quarter broad. I could wish our quality would adopt this modest handsome fashion, and the more, as it would suit the solid genius and character of our nation, which is not quite so prone to glare and foppery, as the people of some neighbouring Kingdoms.

Devotion, at *Naples*, is very much the mode in Lent; at this season they atone for past negligencies, by many religious assiduities, and even frequenting sermons, which are left chiefly to the middling and poor people the rest of the year; but, previously to Lent, during three weeks or a month, there is a species of devotion to be seen here, almost peculiar to
Naples,

Naples, either not being known, or, at least, not much practised in the other cities of *Italy*. This is a dedication of a *Presepio* to the Blessed Virgin, and the Infant *Jesus*, in many of their churches, and many of their private houses. A *Presepio* properly signifies a manger, and as our Saviour was immediately after his birth deposited in a manger, the construction of a *Presepio* was designed in honour of that event. It is a group of little figures, or puppets, representing the whole transaction. There are the Wise Men of the East, with a star over their heads, on one spot: The shepherds attending their flocks, with the Angel descending towards them on another: The Virgin, the Infant, *Joseph*, and the ass, on another. In short, the composer has introduced such figures and historical facts into the group, as the New Testament, and sometimes his own genius have suggested. But what renders a *Presepio* really an object for a man of taste, is the artful disposition of the figures, amidst a scenery of perspective, most wonderfully deceitful to the eye. A certain merchant has one on the top of his house, where the perspective is so well preserved, that, by being open at one end, the distant country and mountains become a continuity of the *Presepio*, and seem really to be a part of it. It is said it cost five hundred pounds but a few years since. A nobleman here had one, where so much silver, and so many beautiful scenes were admitted into the work, that it was valued at eight thousand pounds. This nobleman was expensive in other articles, besides that of his devotion, and was at last obliged to part with his silver *Presepio* to satisfy his creditors. The poor people, if they are not already provided with a *Presepio*, purchase a cheap trumpery one at this season, which, with care, and locking up the remainder of the year, will last them their lives.

I am, Sir, &c.

LETTER XXXVI.

Naples, *March* 1766.

SIR,

WE purpose soon to set out for *Rome*, in order to see the ceremonies, or, as they are stiled in this country, the functions of the Holy Week. You may imagine where
the

the Pope and Cardinals are, the fineſt ſpectacles will be exhibited; but there is a kind of rivalſhip amongſt the cities of *Italy* at this ſeaſon, and one would think each was endeavouring to exceed the other in folly and ſuperſtition. At *Naples* they have a practice unknown at *Rome*, and which is meant as a piece of devotion, a compliment to the Saviour of the World. From the *Friday* to the *Sunday* incluſive, which three days our Lord remained interred in the earth, the quality all viſit in chairs, and thoſe of inferior rank, walk. No carriages are allowed at that time to paſs the ſtreets, leſt by their clatter they ſhould diſturb our Saviour in his grave, I am aware, a ſenſible Catholic, and a ſcholar, will upbraid me with the groſſneſs of this repreſentation, will tell me the ceremony is purely allegorical, and that there is not a living mortal ſo ſtupid as to imagine they really can diſturb the reſt of our Saviour, whom they know to have riſen the third day after he deſcended into the grave. I confeſs this kind of argument might have made ſome impreſſion on me, had I never come into theſe countries; but here I ſee that mankind is incapable of allegory. Place before them an image to remind them of the deity, and they prefently fall down and worfhip the image itfelf; fo, at *Naples*, I perceive there are thoufands who do not reafon and refine, but underftand this ceremony in its plain, obvious, literal fenfe.

Amongft other ridiculous practices, which are meant as facred ones, they faften a man on a crofs, and carry him in proceffion through the ftreets of *Naples*. On each fide of the crofs are two vulgar women, who, with their hair difhevelled, and fome geftures of lamentation, reprefent *Mary* and *Mary Magdalen* in tears. The man who reprefents our Saviour on the crofs, is fome poor fellow, who is paid a fhilling or two for his trouble, the extenfion of his arms for a length of time being very uneafy and painful to him. As I never faw this function myfelf, I fhall not enter into a farther detail; fuffice it to fay, it has an irreligious tendency: The perfonages who reprefent, are too infignificant to fupport the dignity of the defign, and the mob, inftead of efteeming it an awful folemn emblem, every now and then break out into ludicrous mockeries upon *Jefus* and the two *Marys*, to the great fcandal of true religion.

They

LETTER XXXVI.

They have even admitted into their devotion, the noise and explosion of gunpowder. I was roused one day from my seat, by an universal discharge of the artillery of *Naples*. Had an enemy been near, I should have been terrified: In the present posture of affairs I was only curious; and, to my great surprize, was informed the guns had been fired for the immaculate conception of the Virgin *Mary*: In truth, the *Neapolitans* are the most gunpowder nation in the world: A merchant does not send a few barrels of wine into the city, but that the carriages are preceded by squibs, crackers, and muskets; then, what is worse, during the *Christmas* week, all the young men, boys, and little children, spend every farthing they can scrape together, in gunpowder, and pop and shoot all day, and all night, to the great annoyance of those in health, as well as those in sickness; but it is an evil not to be redressed, because it is esteemed a religious act done in honour of the season.

I am, Sir, &c.

LETTER XXXVII.

NAPLES, *March* 1766.

SIR,

I MAKE no doubt that you are apprised the *Italians* count their hours till twenty-four o'clock; but I shall inform you of some particulars on this subject, which, I presume, you are not acquainted with. They do not reckon as we do, from the moment the sun is in its meridian, or, in other words, from noon, but they begin their account from the time it is almost, and not quite dark; which instant of time varying every day, renders this reckoning very inconvenient, vague, and perplexed. For example; if to-day they begin to count from our six o'clock in the evening, it will be one with them, when it is seven with us; but to-morrow at our seven, it will with them exceed one, by as many minutes as the day is lengthened. To obviate, therefore, this error in time, they alter their clocks and watches as often as the error amounts to fifteen minutes, advancing, or putting them back, as the days shorten or lengthen: However, if a man forget to alter

his

his watch on the appointed day, he loses or gains a quarter of an hour, and cannot be very punctual to his engagements. I hope I have stated this matter in such a light, as to make you entirely master of it.

In this Southern latitude, the days are neither so short in winter, nor so long in summer as with us. The shortest day in the year is nine hours ten minutes long, that is, the sun sets at thirty-five minutes after four, and they begin their reckoning from five minutes after five, allowing an interval of half an hour, after sun-setting, which is very near the whole twilight. The longest day in the year is but fifteen hours; that is, the sun sets at half an hour after seven, and they begin their reckoning at eight, the twilight in this country lasting but little more than half an hour after sun-set on the 20th of *June*. A man, however, who would be critically exact as to time, should be furnished with proper tables of calculation, because they do not reckon always from just half an hour after sun-set, but vary the reckoning from twenty-seven to thirty-one minutes, as I find by these tables. If one did not know, from much experience, how difficult it is to change established customs, it

would

would be natural to exclaim against the absurdity of this people, in not adopting *English* and *French* clocks, where the utility is so notorious. At *Turin* there are two *English* clocks: There are also two publick ones here, and one or two in most of the great cities in *Italy*; but I observe the natives of the lower sort do not comprehend them; so far are they yet from preferring this kind of reckoning. You will be surprised when I tell you, that I cannot find one learned man here, who knows the origin of this method of reckoning, though I have consulted some, who, I thought, should have been masters of the subject.

The long twilight in *England*, during the summer, is one of the chief pleasures of our climate, and I at first pitied the *Neapolitans* that they were so soon involved in darkness after sun-set, till I reflected on the benefits of this providential contrivance in the frame of the world; for, had it been possible that the structure of the globe could have admitted of the oblique descent of the sun, in these hot countries, as it does in our Northern regions, the poor inhabitants would, in a manner, have been parched, or, rather, this portion of
the

LETTER XXXVII.

the world muſt have been uninhabited; but the ſudden ſetting of the ſun, not allowing in the long days of any conſiderable twilight, the night becomes long, and the intemperate heats are inſtantly ſucceeded by a cooling freſhneſs. This freſhneſs of the evening and night is ſo comfortable during the ſummer ſeaſon, that the *Neapolitan* Gentry often live out of bed the whole night, and ſleep in the extreme heat of the day.

Now I have mentioned the heat, I cannot help obſerving, that, to a man in health, the climate of *England*, with its fogs and cold, ſhould appear preferable to that of *Naples*, where the ſummers, by all deſcription, are ſo grievouſly burning, that, were it an accident that happened but once in thirty or forty years, they might poſſibly call it a plague. They ſit in chairs, with only a thin callico gown, for hours together, ſome days, wholely occupied in wiping off the ſweat that runs in channels down their bodies. Is not cold, with a good fire, a more deſirable ſituation? The winters here, excepting that ſometimes the immoderate rains render them melancholy, are exceedingly pleaſant and wholeſome; for, notwithſtanding the rain,

you

you see no damps on their stair-cases, nor on the walls of their chambers; their iron does not rust as with us, nay, the paintings on the outside of buildings in fresco, remain for years. The season has been much colder than usual, and I have heard some of the *English* assert such a day to be as cold as any day he ever felt in *England*, but then I have heard another declare that same day to be as warm as our first of *May*; so little can we depend upon one another, and so violently affected are we, generally, by our different feelings for the present moment. Take along with you, as some measure, however, of the moderateness of the winter, in comparison of ours, that the flies are not all gone into winter quarters, and, I believe, in *England*, we sometimes see the last of them in *November*. *Naples* would not be so cold as it is, if it were not environed with very high mountains, at the distance, some of twenty-five, others of twenty and fifteen miles, which, together, form an amphitheatre, except in that part where the Bay opens. These mountains, towards the North, North-East, and East, are, in dry winters, often covered with snow, and when the wind blows over them, *Naples* feels the effects: It therefore,

therefore, often happens, that, on the same day, you are scorched by the heat of the sun, and frozen by these penetrating winds, which I suppose, must frequently produce various disorders. I cannot dismiss this subject, without informing you, that Mount *Vesuvius* stands in the midst of this amphitheatre, on a plain, which has given rise to an opinion amongst the naturalists, that, originally, the whole amphitheatre was flat, and that the mountain was formed by an eruption from the bowels of the earth. Notwithstanding I speak of the temperateness of the winter in this climate, yet the present year has exhibited the tops of the abovementioned mountains very frequently covered with snow, and, sometimes the setting sun shining upon the snow, has afforded a most glittering prospect.

 I should have told you, when I mentioned, in a former letter, the custom of exposing their corpses in the procession of funerals, that the people of condition are carried in coffins, as with us, except officers of distinction, who are exposed on a bier, like the common people; but I do not know the reason of the exception.

I am, dear Sir, &c.

LETTER XXXVIII.

NAPLES, *March* 1766.

SIR,

I AM now looking forwards towards *England* and next *December*, when perhaps the cold weather may make me regret the mild winters of *Naples*, but, I am perfuaded, will never make me wifh myfelf there upon the only terms a man can get there; I mean, to travel fo great a diftance, either by land or by fea. I have a notion few men accommodate themfelves better than myfelf, to the little inconveniencies and difficulties which muft occur; but I own to you, were I to remain long in *Italy*, the profpect would be uncomfortable. I think I fhall love *England* the better for having quitted it: I am fure I fhall always entertain a higher opinion of the people there, for this excurfion. Perhaps it is a kind providence which, (according to our quaint proverb) makes *Home, home, &c.* but really and impartially, there are in *England* more bleffings, more fweets of life, and more virtues, in my opinion, than are generally met with in other countries. Even the climate, bad

bad as it is in winter, when compared with the intemperate heats of the summer season here, is preferable to that of *Naples*. An asthmatic man will contradict this assertion, but a man in good health will say with *Charles* II. " There is not a kingdom in the world " where a man can walk in the streets more " days in a year, nor more hours in the day, " than in *England*." Both the rains and the heat in this country are sometimes immoderately tedious. A certain *Neapolitan*, with whom I have contracted a friendship, has, for many years, kept an account of the rain, which he tells me, falls to the quantity of thirty or thirty-one inches in a twelvemonth; now, if I remember exactly, there fall only from nineteen to twenty-two inches in *London*; the difference, therefore, of this kind of bad weather, in the two cities, is prodigious.

The news-papers have told you, that the winter at *Naples* has been extremely severe, but you must remember, it has been only so by comparison, for the flies have not been so pinched, but that some of them have kept out the whole time; a very sure criterion of the moderateness of the cold. I cannot drop this subject, without observing, that I have not seen

seen one of our young gentlemen on his travels, who does not appear more eager than I am to return to his friends and country. I had always figured to myself, that they were in the highest delight when making the Grand Tour; but I find by experience, that when they are here, they consider it as a kind of apprenticeship for qualifying a gentleman, and would often return abruptly, did they not feel themselves ashamed to indulge the inclination: Indeed, were it not, that in the great cities they meet with numbers of their countrymen, the hours would lie too heavily on their hands; for few men can spend their whole life in the pursuit of virtú, and some have not the qualifications of birth to recommend them to persons of high rank, where only is to be found what little society there is in *Italy*. It must be confessed, the nobility here are not only polite to *Englishmen*, but almost proud of their company, provided they come with a testimony that they have blood in their veins, or are gentlemen of large fortunes; yet, upon the whole, their *converzationi*, as they are called, grow tiresome, being so little diversified, in comparison of the elegant amusements of *London*. One may easily conceive how

limited

LETTER XXXVIII.

limited a conversation must be, where men dare not speak on the subject, of liberty, politics, or religion; and where no drama is exhibited, and very few writings, except of the most ridiculous, abject, superstitious kind are published; so that a man, in a liberal way of thinking, has no refuge in these conversations but cards, where, Scandal says, there is much foul play; and, probably, Scandal speaks truth; for I have heard of many young gentlemen who have lost considerably, but I never heard of one who carried off his trunk full of sequins.

The race of men in this city, seem, in my eyes, more robust and athletic than the run of mankind in *London*, and I am told that they carry larger burdens here than ours can do. When I reflect on the wretched nourishment with which the poor children are fed here, and how miserably fallow and bloated they appear during their infancy, I cannot but say I am astonished at this phænomenon; though, perhaps, the climate of this country naturally produces stouter men than that of *England*; or, possibly, all those who have not very good stamina perish, and the stout ones only survive, which may serve as a kind of solution of this extraordinary fact. I am very much disposed to account for it in this manner, because, notwithstanding the great numbers of children in this city, as all the lower people marry, they would swarm still more, were they not carried off under two years of age in a much greater proportion than amongst us.

The other day I saw a fellow six feet high, and very brawny, assault another with his fist, but in so aukward and womanly a manner as made not only me but the ladies laugh. Were you to see such a man at *Broughton*'s, you would bet on his head, whoever were his antagonist; but, I dare say, an *Etonean* boy of seventeen or eighteen would have boxed him to a jelly. I never had a good opinion of this *English* practice of boxing till I came to *Italy*; but I now find it is an innocent and laudible fashion; for men must have some kind of vent for their indignation, some salvo for their honour; and it is happy, when the worst thing a man does in his wrath, is the giving a slap on the face, or a punch in the stomach, to the offending party: Here, angry men immediately have recourse to the knife, and stab in an instant. It is amazing how many assassinations there are in *Italy*, almost

LETTER XXXVIII.

most all of them the effects of quarrels. Now, none of these assassinations would take place, were the good *English* mode of boxing introduced amongst them. I was much pleased, when I dined with *Voltaire*, to hear a remark of his on the common people of *England:* Some *Frenchmen*, unpolitely enough, in my presence, took occasion to sneer at the whole nation, on the account of this custom amongst the common people. *Voltaire*, with great vivacity, vindicated, in some degree, the practice. "You may ridicule, said he, if you please, the manners of an' *English* mob; but, in the very instance you have pitched upon, they shew a species of honour not known in any other part of the world;" and then appealed to me, whether it were not true, that when two fellows fight in the street, if one throw down the other, the standing combatant do not permit his antagonist to rise, and come to a second attack, scorning to take any base advantage of him in that predicament; nay, continued he, is not this generous principal so well established amongst the mob, that were a revengeful man, by chance, to attempt any unfair cruelty, whilst he was superior, the spectators would fly to the relief of the diſtreſſed combatant, and place him on his legs again, in ſpite of his triumphant adverſary? You may imagine I gave my aſſent to this panegyrick, and was not a little delighted to ſee the tables turned in favour of *Engliſhmen*.

It has always been ſaid, that the guardians of a pupil King, endeavour to keep their ward in ignorance, as a means to preſerve their own power when he comes of age. The *Neapolitan* regency ſeems to have adopted this golden rule. Would you believe, that tho' the King be turned of fifteen, and is contracted to a daughter of the Queen of *Hungary*, his tutors ſuffer him to play with puppets, and are not aſhamed to let ſtrangers, and all the world ſee, in what his principal amuſement conſiſts? In one of the chambers of the palace, you find *Punch*, and the whole company of Comedians, hanging upon pegs, and cloſe to them is a little theatre, where they are exhibited, not to the Monarch, but by the Monarch.

At *Rome* and *Naples*, during the Holy Week, there are ſeveral religious, or, if you pleaſe, ſuperſtitious ceremonies performed; and the King here, becauſe he cannot with

pro-

propriety partake of the publick communion, has, juſt by *Punch*'s Theatre, on the ſame floor, a little piece of ſcenery, as long as a dining table, which is to be lighted up with candles as thick as packthread; and here the Function of burying our Saviour is to be performed, for his entertainment and devotion, in a few days.

Every *Friday*, during the month of *March*, there is a faſhion in *Naples* for the gentry to go in proceſſion to a certain church, about a mile out of the city, in their fineſt coaches, and many of them with ſix horſes, and a ſeventh on the off hand, between the two foremoſt pair, ornamented with jingling bells. I was at this ceremony yeſterday, and was much ſurpriſed to ſee ſo prodigious a quantity of equipages; for though I am perſuaded many keep their coaches here, who dine upon ſtewed cabbage, yet the concourſe vaſtly exceeded my expectation; for I can confidently affirm, that upon no occaſion whatſoever, either in *London* or in *Paris*, have I ſeen near ſo great a number.

I am, Sir, &c.

LETTER XXXIX.

NAPLES, *March* 1766.

SIR,

SERMONS are not the purfuit of the gentry in Catholick countries, and good preachers are therefore uncommon. I had rafhly flattered myfelf I fhould have gathered much fruit from the pulpit, or at leaft, that I fhould have been entertained. At this feafon of the year, preachers of the moft diftinguifhed parts quit their convents, and fpread themfelves through the great cities of *Italy*, to inftruct the people, and difplay their own talents. You may imagine fuch a capital as *Naples* invites fome of the moft eminent amongft them. Thefe I have followed; but, as I have hinted, am difappointed and mortified. A foreigner cannot be too cautious in forming an opinion on the declamation, either of the ftage or the pulpit: In every country, there is a different tone peculiar to that country, which it requires a man fhould be born there, to tafte and to feel; fo that what is fweetnefs to a native, is diffonance to a ftranger. Making therefore an allowance for the chant of *Italian* eloquence, and supposing that their sing song manner of preaching be persuasive and masculine, I will endeavour to assign other reasons why I am mortified.

The picture of St *Paul* preaching at *Athens*, and the comparison (so common) of his attitude, with the action of the *Italian* preachers, had given me great prejudices in their favour: I had not conceived, till I was brought to the experiment, how dangerous it is to attempt much action, which, to be graceful, demands the nicest guidance. Some of the pulpits here, are a kind of gallery, which allow great scope for action: The injudicious preachers do not fail to take the advantage of it; very often in the heat of their discourse running from one end to the other; and it is this excess, this abuse of action, which I object to. It is the habit of this country to employ much action in the most trivial conversations: This habit infests the bar and the pulpit, and, from an indiscriminate application of it, on slight occasions, the force and effect of it is lost on great ones. We see upon the stage, where action is studied, how few know how to adapt it to the sentiment and
degree

degree of passion they are to express; no wonder, therefore, if the generality of preachers, men bred up in a monastery, far from the circle of the polite world, and perhaps, under the influence of a superstitious enthusiasm, should be deficient in an art of so delicate a nature. You see my opinion is, that, however powerful action may be, when restrained within the bounds of decorum and good sense, it becomes unpleasant and disgustful when it runs into boisterousness, as is too frequently the case in *Italy*.

But what gives me more offence still, is, a familiarity of stile which they have introduced into their compositions, when even God Almighty and our Saviour are the subject in question. I went the other day to hear the most celebrated preacher now in *Naples*, who, amongst other inelegancies, gave us a familiar dialogue, in a very familiar manner, betwixt God and *Jesus Christ*, in which our Saviour begg'd and pray'd him that he would not damn mankind; but God being inexorable, and deaf to all intreaty, our Saviour said, " Why then if your justice must exceed your mercy, be so good to damn me and spare them." This the preacher told us God was *so good* to comply

comply with. I believe I have not miftaken him a jot, becaufe another Gentleman, who was prefent, agreed with me in every particular, word for word, and I was fo fearful of mifreprefenting the truth, that I immediately committed it to paper. Now, if I do not abufe your confidence, and if this preacher be in the higheft eftimation, as I believe he is, in what a ftate of barbarifm muft the pulpit be at this juncture!

There has crept alfo into fafhion, an idle cuftom of telling a ftory in their fermons, with which they fometimes finifh their difcourfe, as our clergy do with a practical inference. It is true, the moral of their ftories is meant to be a religious one; but their attempts to tell them in the character of a fine Gentleman, and a man of the world, you will readily imagine muft often mifcarry. A certain Catholick Lady informed me, that laft year fhe was at church, when a celebrated Jefuit told the following ftory.—" That Queen *Elizabeth*, fo famous throughout the world for her herefy, made a compact with the Devil, that if he would indulge her in all fhe defired, and fuffer her to reign fo many years, fhe would furrender her foul at the conclufion

of

of that term." Accordingly, the day she died, there was a great black cloud ascended from the *Thames*, which drew the attention of an infinite number of spectators, who, at last, heard a voice from the cloud pronounce these words, *I am the soul of Queen* Elizabeth, *now going to the Devil for the sins I have committed.* There is one week in Lent, that most of the Ladies of distinction go to hear a sermon every day in the above-mentioned church, and it was on one of those days, the Jesuit told this story to the politest congregation in *Naples*.

The preachers here, have a crucifix, about two feet high, sticking close to their elbow, in the pulpit, but moveable at pleasure. The *Christ* upon it has, generally, a crown of thorns, and the streams of blood down his face and breast are painted with a lively red. At the conclusion of the sermon, or on any other apposite occasion, when the preacher is to set forth the sufferings and agonies of our Saviour, dying for the salvation of the world, he takes the crucifix in his hands, and displays the bleeding wounds of the image, when, if he have any pathetic powers, he never fails to extort from the audience such marks of contrition

tion and horror, such knockings on the breast, such an effusion of tears, and, sometimes, amongst the women, such involuntary hysterical screams, as you Protestants have no idea of; so forcibly is the soul acted on when the eyes are the instruments by which it feels, and not the ears only. The adopting such a crucifix for that use in *England*, would be a dangerous experiment; but, were it practised, I would defy any of the audience to sleep, as they do now a days, in Protestant churches.

Powerful as the crucifix usually is, particularly in the hands of an eloquent priest, I am tempted to tell you a ludicrous story, bordering upon prophaneness, where its efficacy failed; it is one of those instances where a burning zeal, through a deplorable ignorance, furnishes matter of raillery to scoffers, and compassion to such who are truly religious.—
" At *Naples* there is a place called the *Largo del Castello*, not unlike our *Tower-Hill*, the resort of the idle populace. Here, every afternoon, Monks and Mountebanks, Pickpockets and Conjurors, follow their several occupations. The Monk (for I never saw more than one at a time) holds forth, like our itinerant field-preachers, to what congregation

gation he can collect; the Mountebank, by means of Punch, and his fellow comedians, endeavours to gather as great an audience as he can. It happened one day, that Punch succeeded marvellously, and the poor Monk preached to the air, for not a living creature was near him: Mortified and provoked that a puppet-shew, within thirty yards of him, should draw the attention of the people from the Gospel to such idle trash, with a mixture of rage and religion he held up the crucifix, and called aloud, *Ecco il vero Pulcinella ;—* "*Here is the true* Punchinello,—*come here,* "—*come here !*"—The story is so well known in *Naples* to be true, that the most devout people tell it; and, were it not for such a sanction, I should hardly have repeated it.

I am, Sir, &c.

LETTER XL.

ROME, *March* 21, 1766.

SIR,

WE arrived laſt night, in good health at this place, after a diſagreeable journey, if ſuch a thing be poſſible, when the weather is as fine as you can conceive it. We took another road for our return, but both in our going to, and coming from *Naples*, our views were ſo circumſcribed by the adjacent mountains, that, were *Italy* to take its character from the proſpects, or the ſoil, in this rout, the proudeſt *Roman* could not have called it the *Garden of the World*; for all theſe mountains are exceedingly barren. I ſhould mention, however, that the ſoil in the valleys is very rich, and really, in general, ſo exempt from ſtones, or clay, that I had been many months here before I ſaw a man uſe a common ſpade, the implement for digging being the iron part of a ſpade, faſtened to a long handle, and worked like a hoe; which, you may imagine, is an expeditious method, where the ſoil is ſoft, but would be impracticable where it is ſtiff with clay, or clogged with ſtones.

In travelling through the kingdom of *Naples*, and the Ecclesiastical State, an *Englishman* is struck at the scarcity of villages and cottages; indeed one may almost assert, that there is no such thing as a village, or even a cluster of houses approaching to the resemblance of a village; what single separate houses there are, you see at a small distance from the towns; accordingly, as the country is so thinly inhabited, you find the towns swarming with inhabitants, most of which, I suppose, walk forth every day, to the distance of several miles, to labour in the country, I mean such who do labour; for there are multitudes of these idle people, who wrap themselves up in their cloaks, and stand pensively stupid in the streets from morning to night. Holydays, which are very frequent in this country, present an appearance very disagreeable to my eyes, that is, every soul in this sauntering attitude.

The towns stand on the summit of a hill, and, at some distance, afford a pleasant prospect; being built with stone, and having flat roofs; but, when you enter within the walls, and see the houses so offensively nasty, and not only without glass, but even without shutters,

ters, the marks of dirty poverty are so strong, that they almost turn the stomach. Some of the inns on this road exceed in filth and bad accommodations all that I have ever written on that subject before: I do sincerely believe, that they no more think of wiping down a cobweb in a bed-chamber, than our farmers do of sweeping them away in an old barn; and can assure you, upon my honour, that were a spider ever to fall from his mansion, every guest would be liable to receive it in his face, as he lies in bed; for the whole cieling is covered with them; and, as I have lain on my back, philosophically speculating on their numbers, it has been matter of wonder how nature should have provided for their subsistence, since the whole nation of flies hardly seems a sufficient sustenance for so many beasts of prey.

My constant degree of asthma would not suffer me to ascend Mount *Vesuvius* to the very top, so as to take a survey of its opening, or, as it is called, the *crater*; and, perhaps, it may have been well for my bones that I could not attempt it; for the party with which I should probably have made the expedition, but narrowly escaped with their lives.

lives. Mr ——, Mr ——, and Mr ——, on *Tuesday* se'nnight, notwithstanding the menaces of the mountain, which, at present, is in a blustering state, had the curiosity to see all that could be seen, and were not intimidated enough, by some small eruptions, to withdraw till they had indulged their speculation, when the mountain poured out such a quantity of large stones, that it is wonderful they were not overwhelmed and demolished. Mr —— received a wound in his arm, which has been attended with some alarming circumstances, and confined him a considerable time. Mr —— received a large contusion on the calf of his leg, which, however, will do him no mischief. Mr —— was not hurt; but a stone was hurled against his walking-stick, with such velocity as to carry it out of his sight. After this accident, nobody will go up the mountain till it become more pacific, and, probably, that will not happen before it be delivered of the burthen with which it now groans.

Last *Saturday* I went up with some gentlemen to the Hermitage, which is as high as horses or mules can carry a man; it is inhabited by a *French* hermit turned of seventy, who

who sells wine, and makes a profit of travellers. In that cell, you are too far off to be annoyed by the stones, and have a very fine view of the most fertile country in *Europe*; the city, the bay, and the adjacent islands making together a most beautiful prospect. When you are at the Hermitage, you discover more clearly the true shape of the burning mountain, which is evidently a distinct mountain, very steep, placed on another, which rises with a gradual ascent as far as the foot of this distinct mountain, that is to say, as high as the Hermitage; the whole surface of the inferior one is covered with vineyards, except in certain channels where the streams of *lava* have run down when the mountain boiled over: Some of these vineyards produce the wine called *Lachrimæ Christi*.

I believe, I need not now explain to you, that the *lava* is that matter which is melted within the bowels of the mountain, and is thrown out by the eruptions, and which, when grown cold, assumes the nature of stone. From the Hermitage, all the way up to the summit, the mountain is covered either with ashes, or *lava*, and, being excessively steep, is ascended with the greatest difficulty, by the assistance of guides accustomed to it; some of which, going before, draw you up by a string fastened round them; and others, pushing behind, forward the motion. By the best informations I can get, the gentlemen were, with all these aids, betwixt one and two hours arriving to the top; so perpendicular is the rising, and so slippery is the footing. I should not say slippery, but rather loose, being ashes, or sand, which gives so much way, that, though you advance your foot twenty-four inches, the weight of your body makes it sink almost to the place from which you advanced, so that you gain but very little way every step. What gave me the greatest pleasure, in this day's pursuit, were the explosions within the cavity, which very much resembled the noise of a proof of cannon at *Woolwich*, heard at a little distance; they were at times very frequent, and one of the gentlemen who was with us, counted, by his moment hand watch, eight explosions in fourteen seconds. I confess, amongst the operations of nature, hardly any ever affected me more with the idea of grandeur, than this. I wish I had good lungs, and there had been

less

less danger in peeping; for, I am sorry not to have seen the whole wonder of this phœnomenon. You, at a distance, perhaps hold this infernal mountain in some horror, but the people in the neighbourhood, I mean the curious, consider it as an amusing object; and the Hermit, with great exultation, and a caper, told us, we should certainly have an eruption this year; *Ah Messieurs, disoit il, certainment nous aurons de la lave cette année.*

N. B. The Hermit's prediction was fulfilled a few days after I left *Naples*, when the mountain boiled over most plentifully.

I am, Sir, &c.

LETTER. XLI.

ROME, *March* 23, 1766.

SIR,

I Have been this morning *(Palm Sunday)* at the Pope's Chappel, to see one of the ceremonies of this season, called here a Function. I question whether the account of it be worth the time you will spend in reading it; so much mummery, farce, and pageantry, one would have thought impossible to be introduced

troduced into any religion, if we had not seen it introduced into so many. The Function of to day, was the Benediction of the Palm Branches, carried in procession afterwards, by the Cardinals, Bishops, Penitentials of St *Peter*'s, Prelates, (a different appellation here from Bishops) Generals of Orders, Cavalieri dei Cardanali, (Cardinal's Gentlemen) and other classes of men, admitted into this ceremony, down to the foreigners, who all may, if they please, and some did, receive a blessed Palm-branch from the Pope's hand, and kiss the hem of his garment.

I came into *Italy* with an opinion, that the finest music in the world, and the finest performers, were procured for the Pope's chapple; guess how much I was surprised to be told, that a Pope never admits any other instrument than an organ, and generally hears vocal music only. The office, therefore, began by singing, without music, in the manner of our psalm-singing in *England*, for the first time I ever heard it in a Catholic country. This did not last above five or six minutes, when the proper officers presented to his Holiness, an implement, which, viewed at a distance,

tance, resembles one of our beef-eater's halberts, but is composed of a kind of water-flag, interwoven, so as to be knotted a little, like a pine-apple, and, for want of real Palms, is understood to be a Palm. After blessing this instrument, the Pope delivers it into the hands of the Cardinals, Bishops, &c. so there are as many Blessings and Palms, as there are Cardinals, &c. Upon receiving the blessed Palm, they kneeled and kissed it, and then kissed the garment of his Holiness at about the height of his knee; but when the Prelates, and the orders below them, received the Palm, the proper officer gave them notice, as I observed, to kiss the hem of his garment near the ground. After these benedictions of the Palms, and the distribution of them, which was very tedious, lasting fifty minutes, without the least variation in the ceremony, except that the lower classes, instead of the implement I have just described, received only a small branch of a tree, they all walked in procession, with the Palms in their hands, the Cardinals first, and the Pope last, who was carried on the shoulders of twelve men, in an elbow-chair. As he passed along, we all prostrated ourselves, and received his

Bene-

Benediction both in going out, and returning into the chapel. After this, Mass was celebrated by the Pope's nephew. I should have told you, that no *Englishman* presented himself to the Pope, nor do I think it would be decent for Protestants to do so publick an act, were there no other objection than the risk of giving offence to rigid Catholics, who, probably, would suppose it mockery and ridicule in a Heretick.

I am now in a country where the Sovereign is a Priest; at a time of the year too, when the priesthood displays all its pomp, not to call it arrogance; and, I assure you, it is a trial for the patience of reason. We very well know, from the history of the church, what tyrants they have been formerly, before the laity dared to assume the prerogatives of civil liberty; and, that they do not yet abate one jot of their presumption, you may learn from a passage or two I lately met with in a book printed at *Naples*, since the commencement of the present century. Believe my candour and veracity, when I give you my word that I do not strain the sense in the translation. —In a chapter upon the article of Confessors, the author (a Priest) says, *A Confessor partakes*

takes both of the nature of God and of man; with God, he is a man; with man, he is a God.—Again, *Jesus Christ, to absolve man, suffered infinite agonies, and even death itself, whilst a Confessor, by only lifting up his hands, acquits the guilty sinner.*

The Pope and his Council have come to a resolution, upon the death of the Pretender, to have no more concern in this business, and not only do not acknowledge the title of the present Pretender, but have forbidden all the Princes and Cardinals here to visit him; so that he sees only two or three friends, and leads a recluse and melancholy life. We this morning saw him at St *Peter's* church; he came thither, attended by three Gentlemen, and seven servants, to pay his devotions; there was hardly one in the church but ourselves, so that we had the opportunity of examining his person and behaviour very minutely. When I first saw him on his knees, I felt some compunction, which went off by degrees, as I became more certain, from his gestures, of the extreme bigotry and superstitious turn of his mind. After he had prayed at one altar, (for it was not to hear mass) he walked to another, and prayed a second time,

kneeling in both places on the hard pavement. I never saw any one more stedfast in prayer than he appeared, not allowing his eyes to wander one moment from either the altar, the ground, or the book in his hand. During this transaction, reason superseded my pity, and I felt a kind of exultation in reflecting we were not under the dominion of a Prince so fond of images and hierarchy. Now I have seen him before the *Virgin Mary*, I can believe all that was said of his gross attachment to Popery when he was with us in 1745. His revenues are said to be very straight, not exceeding four thousand pounds a year. His stature is very elegant, but his face is a little bloated and pimpled, as if he had drunk too much, a vice laid to his charge, but, perhaps, without good grounds. I am told, his brother, the Cardinal, resents the conduct of this court more than he himself does, perhaps his heart is more set upon propagating the true faith in the realms of *Great-Britain*; for, however enthusiastic the Prince, as he was called, may be in his persuasion, the Cardinal is much more so; and, possibly, he may think his brother deprived of all hopes by this step. I have had some conversation with
a very

LETTER XLI.

a very sensible Ecclesiastick here, who knows every thing which passes, both in the Pope's and the Pretender's palace. I asked, what name the Pretender goes by at present? to which he could hardly give an answer, as he says they so strictly observe the prohibition not to stile him King, that he is never mentioned; or if, by chance, they are obliged to speak of him, it is under the absurd appellation of Prince of *Wales*.

I forbore to finish the detail of the Function I saw at the Pope's chapel, because I would not give you any of my suggestions for matter of fact; but now I am fully informed. I told you, the Pope, Cardinals, &c. went in procession out of the chapel, with their palm-branches in their hands, into an adjacent great hall, but did not mention the whole form, because I was not master of the words set to musick, and sung by two Eunuchs, upon shutting the chapel-door, the moment the procession had entered the hall. The words were these, (the very same I had suggested) *Lift up your heads, O ye gates, that the King of Glory may come in*, &c. upon which the doors flew open, and the procession returned into the chapel.

This

LETTER XLI.

This evening the great Functions will begin at the chapel in the Vatican, when the celebrated *Miserere* will be performed without instrumental musick: Some of the Noblemen will wash the feet of the men pilgrims, and the noble Ladies the feet of the women pilgrims. On *Sunday* next, if I mistake not, the Pope himself, after saying Mass, performs the same ceremony. There is a prohibition, forbidding the presence of women at most of these Functions; but a *Roman* woman of Quality can introduce foreign Ladies into a certain gallery (where men only are supposed to be) without offence, and they are so ready to shew their politeness to the *English* nation, that our Ladies find an easy introduction to them, and, with a proper recommendation, never fail to partake of all the ceremonies.

There are many *English* at *Rome*, most of them gentlemen of fortune, and most of them men who do honour to their country. I know it is a received opinion in *England*, that our youth, who travel, fall immediately into dissipation, and disgrace their country; but I have seen no such examples in *Italy*; perhaps the case is singular, and any other year

year I might have formed a different judgment; but I speak from what I know, and, were I to give an opinion upon that disputable question, *The advantages and disadvantages of travelling*, I should not hesitate to declare, that the benefits are numerous, and that I see no other evil in it than what arises to the nation from the sums expended in foreign parts.

I am, Sir, &c.

LETTER XLII.

ROME, *March* 31, 1766.

SIR,

THE Holy Week, with all its Functions, ended last night. These ceremonies, like the spectacles of the ancient *Romans*, serve to entertain the people, and keep them in good humour, who, otherwise, would be as mutinous in these days for want of bread, as they used to be in the times of the first Consuls. Wherever I travel, I find the multitude discontented with their governors, and I suppose it must be always the case, sometimes

LETTER XLII.

times with, and sometimes without foundation; therefore, some play-thing or another must be thrown out to them to prevent their petulancy. A good Catholick would be shocked to hear me treat these Functions, where they think the Salvation of Souls is concerned, as having a temporal and political use; but we Hereticks, who are denied Grace, esteem it the most favourable construction that can be given to all these raree-shows: A sour *Mahometan*, whose religion consists in prayers, fastings, and ablutions would treat the exhibitions of Saints, Relicks, Virgins, Crucifixes, &c. with more rigour, and call the whole, Profaneness, Blasphemy, and Idolatry.

Last *Thursday* the Pope, according to annual custom, pronounced his Benediction from a balcony in St *Peter*'s, which overlooks the church-yard, where a monstrous croud of people was collected on the occasion. The manner of the form is more suitable to the holiness of his character, than I was aware of; for I had understood, he cursed all Turks, Hereticks, &c. on the face of the earth; whereas, that part of the function is performed by the two Deacons, (Cardinals) who read

the

the Curse, one in *Italian*, the other in *Latin*; and the words are no sooner out of their mouths, than he pronounces the Benediction, and wipes off all the efficacy of the Curse: The Pope is, during the whole ceremony, supported on the shoulders of twelve men, in an armed chair, holding in his hand a large lighted wax taper; and, in the very instant that the last words of the Curse are uttered, the bell tolls, and he throws it down among the people: which circumstance clearly explains the sense of a proverb well known in *England*, of swearing, or cursing, by bell, book, and candle. I had the good fortune to be placed close to his Holiness's elbow; and, whilst he read the blessing, and three or four prayers, or exhortations previous to it, I overlooked the office; and, I confess to you, was edified by the modesty and decorum of the form, as well as by his Holiness's manner of chanting them. The exhortations are of the declaratory kind; that if the assembly would repent sincerely of their sins, and sin no more, there was room for absolution; and the Benediction seemed to be as little arrogant as that pronounced by our Ministers at the end of the Liturgy, viz. *The Grace of our Lord Jesus*

Jesus Christ, &c. In the moment that he is speaking the Benediction, the bells toll, the drums beat, and the cannon at the castle of St *Angelo* fire, which adds to the awefulness of the scene, and renders the performance truely solemn.

Yesterday *(Easter-Sunday)* the same Function was repeated, with this difference, that there was no Curse, but only the Benediction. The concourse of people was greater, all the Peasants from the adjacent countries being more at leisure on a *Sunday*, to come and partake of the blessing. As it is a religious ceremony, and the mob make all their religion consist in ceremony, and a due submission to the church and the priesthood, there are no riots here, as there would be with us; but they are as peaceable and silent from the beginning to the end of the Function, as an elegant audience at *Drury Lane*, when *Garrick* is on the stage. The moment the cannon at St *Angelo* fire, 'the good people in the neighbourhood of *Rome*, who hear them, prostrate themselves, and are supposed to have the benefit of the benediction. There are both days two squadrons of horse, and a small battalion of foot, drawn out before the church,

church, which are not a little ornament to the Feſtival; for, tho' his Holineſs's troops might poſſibly have made no great figure in the fields of *Minden*, they are very well cloathed, and add much to the glory of the day, and the beauty of St *Peter*'s church-yard.

I ſhall not deſcribe any of the other Functions, ſuch as feeding Pilgrims, waſhing their feet by people of quality; and again the ſame ceremony performed by his Holineſs, with Prieſts and Cardinals.

Yeſterday he celebrated Maſs in St *Peter*'s before he pronounced the Benediction, a very tedious and tireſome ſervice both for the poor old man and his congregation; yet theſe things are worth ſeeing once, and were a man to chuſe a month in the year to ſpend at *Rome*, I would recommend that month, in which the Holy Week is included.

I am, Sir, &c.

LETTER XLIII.

Rome, April 7, 1766.

SIR,

YESTERDAY we had another Function, which, I believe, is the last trick we shall see performed by his Holiness. It was a blessing bestowed on about two hundred and thirty Maidens, the greater part of which are to get husbands if they can, and the remainder are to dedicate themselves to a Monastick life; but, besides the cœlestial Benediction, the Pope bestows likewise the Terrestial one, of forty or fifty scudi (an *English* crown) to each maiden; and, what may seem absurd to us *Englishmen*, a double portion to those who take the veil: They make a procession through the streets, dressed all in white, like the ancient *Roman* vestals, to a certain church, where the Pope expects them to kiss his slipper, and receive the good things both of Heaven and Earth at his hands. Those who take the veil, bring up the rear, adorned with a crown of flowers on their heads, and a *Christ* on their bosoms, who, in *Italy*, is called the spouse of these self-denying Virgins. It should

LETTER XLIII.

should seem, that, in the imagination of young maidens, and old Monks, Matrimony is the most flattering of all ideas; for, at the very instant that the Virgin renounces the world, and dedicates herself to celibacy and retirement, I mean at the ceremony of her profession, the priest holds forth sometimes very gayly on this subject; and, though her supposed marriage with *Christ* be allegorical and spiritual, his discourse, I assure you, is often plain and carnal. The girls too, who are designed for the Veil, are kept in very good humour the year before they take it, by conferring on them the endearing title of *Sposina*, that is, the little spouse of *Christ*.

It is worth knowing, that there are at *Rome* many legacies left, and donations given, for this purpose of martying off young women, so that every young woman, with some interest, may hope for a little fortune to furnish a lodging for their outset in the world; but it is only once a year that his Holiness attends on this ceremony. Formerly, before the use of coaches became so common, this was a most shewy anniversary, not only all the Cardinals, but the Princes also, accompanying the Pope on horseback, with their

horses

horses caparisoned in the richest manner. In these distributions, every parish in *Rome* has a certain proportionate interest, sending such or such a number of girls, according to their respective donations. It does not follow, however, that because the girls are entitled to a fortune, they procure a husband; and, what is worse, if they do not get a husband, they renounce the portion: But every young woman in *Rome* has a right to get as many nominations as she can; and there is a poor young Lady here, of a certain family in *Scotland*, who, by the late Chevalier's friendship, procured as many nominations to the several charities of this kind, as amount to two thousand crowns, which she can demand, upon producing a certificate of her marriage.—The spectacle yesterday would have been more curious, if I had remained ignorant of a certain abuse crept into this institution; for it is a practice amongst the young women who are not of the lower class, to depute others, at the expence of two shillings, or two shillings and six-pence, to walk in the procession, and receive the benediction in their stead; the great probability, therefore, of not seeing
the

the individuals who are to be married, deprives the spectators of all the pleasure.

I have mentioned to you, that some of the *Italians* have a due sense of the benefits accruing to their state, from the great sums of money spent by the *English* amongst them. The Governor of *Rome* is in this number, and even his Holiness himself is sometimes pleased to speak with a kind of gratitude on this subject. A very great man here has a *converzatione* every *Sunday* evening, and is very happy to see *English* Gentlemen in the company. I am told he carries his politeness so far as to declare, that, since it is impossible to be an antient *Roman*, could he chuse his birth he would be born an *Englishman*. Some time since, one or two of our countrymen, on some jolly festival, got drunk and mad; ran into the streets, and fell into an unlucky fray, where they drew their hangers, and committed some outrages. The government behaved on this occasion with a gentleness and partiality that ought not to be forgotten. Private intimations were given to the offenders, that they should escape, first doing the justice of making reparation to those who had been outraged. His holiness, who was well informed of every particular, and that it was drunkenness, not cruelty, nor wantonness, which led them into this misbehaviour, was pleased to say, " I have now sat in the chair " so many years, that I have seen at least " four hundred *Englishmen* in that time, and " never heard any complaint against one of " them; yet really, when I consider how " young they are, how distant from controul, " how full of spirits, and how full of money, " I rather wonder, this accident should not " have happened before."

Rome is a much pleasanter city to inhabit, during the fine weather, than *Naples*, as there are many gardens where one may walk, and where custom allows the Ladies to go; notwithstanding that, in general, the *Italian* women hardly know what it is to walk. The chief amusement, through all *Italy*, is their *Corso*, an airing in their coaches, backwards and forwards, in some principal street of their cities, or some avenues of their suburbs, where they make a display of their coaches, horses, and liveries, as we formerly did in *Hyde-Park*. It is a most melancholy entertainment, when considered as the only one; but, for the first time, is a gaudy, and even a pleasing shew;

for

for the *Italians*, as I have said before, spending nothing in race horses, hounds, parliamenteering, &c. reserve their whole income in a manner for their equipages, which, indeed, are more magnificent than you would believe; and those of *Rome* are finer, in my opinion, than any others in this country. There are a prodigious number of palaces here, but they in general rather appear monstrous than grand; and the iron grates before the windows, which are only small panes of dirty glass, in leaden frames, give them all a gloomy aspect, rather resembling prisons than palaces; but what is the greatest disgrace to *Rome*, and, indeed, to every city in *Italy*, is the uncomfortableness and danger of passing through the streets after sun-set; for there is not the least provision made for lighting them. *London* seems to be the single town in *Europe* where that convenience is rightly understood, and carried effectually into execution; for, at *Paris*, the candles in their brown glass lanterns, give but little light whilst they do burn, and, being small, are soon extinguished. It is astonishing this evil should not be reformed, as every night's experience shews how much darkness invites to the perpetration of shameful and attrocious deeds. - Perhaps there is not a more singular proof that the Church presides in this country than that the Cardinals only, are allowed to take flambeaux behind their coaches: All their Princes and Quality are forbidden to use any other light than small lanterns, of which every footman behind the coach carries one.

Protestants, I mean the very good ones, who take all occasions to abuse the Pope, laugh frequently, that his Holiness, in his holy city, should licence brothels; but, if I am well informed, this subject of derision will dwindle in a few years, and quite wear out, the poor whores labouring under so many difficulties and disadvantages, that their numbers and quality diminish daily, there not being, at present, above fifty in all, and most of them a beggarly set of *Neapolitan* outcasts. They are obliged to live at a certain distance from a church, a convent, or any consecrated place; are all registered; a very strict eye is kept over them; and, when they die, they are buried with dogs and hereticks, in unhallowed ground: But what is, perhaps, worse than all this, they must pay, each of them, eighteen-pence a day to an officer, a kind of constable, to watch their conduct, and

and, possibly, to bully for them. I suppose, upon the whole, *Rome* is the chastest city in *Europe*, there being very few publick women, (none for a gentleman) hardly any kept mistresses, and in comparison of all other *Italian* towns, even their Cicesbeos are said, by some, to be innocent; so that such a sober court, as that of his Holiness, has some influence on the manners of the gentry.

Naples, you know, is infamously wicked in this last article, and *Venice* most hellishly wicked, if all that is affirmed be true; in fact, the fashion of Cicesbeos is the most destructive invention for society that I know of. Some volatile inconstant men in *England* are false to the beds of their wives, at the same time that they honour and even love their persons; but this exchange of wives, this marrying one, and associating with another, destroys all affection and regard for the progeny. I intended to have mentioned to you, when I was at *Naples*, for a wonder, that I had seen a mother with a child of seven or eight years old in the chariot with her; but, really, I have been out many days and weeks there without beholding such a phænomenon. How different from the other extreme in *England*, where the fondness of parents crouds their children into every party, and, sometimes, very improperly! Now I am mentioning the comparative sobriety of *Rome*, I should tell you, that his Holiness admits neither of operas, plays, nor balls, during the whole year, except in the Carnival; and, then in order to preserve a greater decorum, and to banish even the appearance, of licentiousness, women are not suffered to represent on that stage, but their characters are performed by beardless youths in womens dresses.

As I did not leave *Naples* before the completion of the Carnival, I have not had the opportunity of seeing the riot of a Carnival at *Rome*. His Holiness allows them but eight days of the time for masking, and on those eight days they have their horse-races, which are so singular in the eyes of an *Englishman*; that though I have not seen them myself, I must give you an account of them from the description of others. None but Princes are entitled to enter these horses; the prize each day is only three ells of a golden, or silver, or velvet embroidered stuff, which the *Jews* of this city, by an antient compact, are obliged to furnish, so that it is of no considerable value; but there is much honour annexed to

the

the victory, and the Prince who wins it, regales the populace with wine and good cheer. The race ground is the *Corso*, the longest street in *Rome*, paved, as all *Rome* is, with a flat stone, but which during the races, if the weather be dry, they strew with dirt to prevent slipperiness: I suppose therefore the nature of this course will surprize you; but how much more will you be astonished when I inform you, that the horses run the race without riders? They are trained to this practice, and being docile animals, they acquire by use, a wonderful degree of cunning; however, like the human species, they have different degrees of understanding, and I am told, some of them in this exercise, shew as much the genius of a jockey, as that of a horse. They contrive to spur them on by pointed instruments, which are hung in such a manner, as to prick their flanks when they are put into action by the motion of the beast. The people of *Rome* have a rage for this pastime, and crowd the narrow street from the starting post to the goal in such numbers, that it is not marvellous, that murder and broken bones should often be the consequence of this diversion. A little beyond the goal, they hang

up

up across the street, at a small distance from each other, two large sheets of cloth, which stop and entangle the horses in their career when the grooms instantaneously seize on them, and in a moment remove the spurs.

I am, Sir, &c.

LETTER XLIV.

ROME, *April* 14, 1766.

SIR,

Notwithstanding the southern latitude of this country, the spring is very backward here, and to a degree that an *Englishman* little expects; this you may imagine is owing to natural causes; but, like all other contrivances of nature, is a very wise and providential one; for as they are, in this mountainous part of the world, subject to cold northern winds in the months of *March* and *April*, were vegetation as much advanced as I should have supposed, their fruits would generally be cut off. I presume, one cause amongst others, which may contribute to retard the spring, is the snow on the adjacent mountains, and, perhaps, the

short-

shortness and the twilight, in the months of *March* and *April*, when compared with ours; though still the season seems to be a fortnight, or, perhaps, three weeks forwarder than with us. As the year advances, the power of the sun increases much faster than in *England*, so that in *July* and *August*, they are three weeks or a month before us.

Rome has not been in such a political uproar these last fifty years as at this present juncture. One would imagine his Holiness had the promise of *Peter*'s pence once more from our side of the water, so devoted does he seem to the court of *England:* Last *Wednesday*, he banished from *Rome*, four heads of Colleges here, for having admitted mass to be said before the Pretender, under the title of King: It certainly was a foolish and rash step in these zealots to fly in the face of government, in so publick and outrageous a manner; and, without a compliment to *England*, it was incumbent on the Pope, in support of his Edict and Prerogative, to make an example of the offenders. The interest of the *Stuart* family, by length of time, seems to be almost worn out in the court of *Rome*; and, at this instant, the power of *England* is considered to

be

be so respectable, that, it is affirmed and believed, the council were unanimous in refusing to acknowledge Mr *Stuart*'s pretensions, and, in consequence of this refusal, they gave out an Ordinance, or Prohibition, to the Cardinals, Princes, &c. forbidding them to see him, but as a private Gentleman; which, in other words, is the same thing as to declare, he shall keep no company but that of his domesticks. It is said, the measures would not have been so severe, had not the Cardinal of *York* behaved, on this occasion, with so unseasonable an obstinacy. It is thought the Pretender himself would have acquiesced and waited for better times; but the Cardinal has been, and continues to be furious; a little more indignation and disloyalty will certainly drive both the brothers from this Asylum. It is reported that the Cardinal, in a memorial he delivered to his Holiness, praying him to acknowledge his brother's title, amongst other arguments, advances that he has nothing to fear from the power of the *English*; for that the present race of *Italians* are not degenerated in the least from their ancestors, the ancient *Romans*. I dont know how the allegation will affect *Englishmen*, but, I assure you, the *Italians* them-

themselves laugh aloud, when they are told the story, so ridiculous does the expression appear to their apprehension.

You may judge, from this system of politicks in the court of *Rome*, that they know as well as you or I, how weak and low at present is the cause of the *Stuart* family, and how much they wish to be well, with *England*. They give out, that they neither can, nor will embroil themselves with a nation which has such long arms (meaning our navy,) but though, perhaps, their fears are groundless in that respect, as I do not imagine (notwithstanding the easy practicability of it) we should have attacked them either at *Civita Vecchia*, or *Ancona*, in case of the acknowledgement; yet the King of *England* has it much in his power to distress the Ecclesiastical State, by discouraging his Nobility and Gentry from coming to *Rome*. If I had not been at *Rome* myself, I could never have conceived in how wretched a condition every kind of business and manufacture is here, so that the ballance of trade is dreadfully in their disfavour; and, it seems to me, that their great resource is the quantity of money spent by the *English*, I do not speak altogether speculatively, for I have

have informed myſelf, that when, by chance, there has been a notable ſcarcity of travellers, the clamours and real want of the trades-people have proved the truth of my ſuggeſtion.

It is with pleaſure I can tell you, that the *Engliſh* ſtudents here, both in painting and ſculpture, have great merit, and are a remarkable ſet of ſober, modeſt men, who, by their decorum, and friendly manner of living amongſt one another, do credit to their profeſſion. It is a pity they ſhould leave this city and their ſtudies; for, as certainly as they arrive at *London*, they will quit their works of genius, and be totally abſorbed in portrait-painting, the ſtumbling-block on which all the *Engliſh* painters fall. It is very poſſible, however, that they will, moſt of them, remain ſome years longer here, as it is of late become a faſhion amongſt our Nobility, to beſpeak copies of ſtatues and picturſs from their countrymen, and they all find employment enough to ſubſiſt comfortably, by this new-invented ſpecies of encouragement, which, with a little ſhare of enthuſiaſm, the common lot of painters, who have any taſte or feeling, will be a ſufficient allurement to keep them in a place where they have continually

nually before their eyes such excellent gratifications. They do, as I am told, earn at their leisure, one hundred pounds a year, each of them, which they esteem equal to three hundred pounds a year in *London*; not that living is three times as cheap here, but because the plan of living is humble and sober at *Rome*, whereas, in *London*, it is dissapation and extravagance. I should therefore hope, that, if the same humour of employing them should continue, they will persist sometime to prosecute their studies, and improve their heads and their hands.

I am now master of all the particulars relating to the banishment of the four superiors, two of which are *Irish*, one *English*, and one *Scotch*. My authority is no less than from the Abbé ——— himself, who was a principal personage in the scene, and lies under an interdict for the part he performed. The Abbé ——— is a very gentleman-like *Scotchman*, residing at *Rome*, and well known to all the *English* Nobility and Gentry, who come thither: His life seems a pleasant one, as he is of consequence enough to be entertained by them all, on the footing of an equal. He is very courteous and happy in the opportunity

tunity of instructing them, and is fully qualified to give a stranger all the lights a curious man could wish for, in every thing relating both to antient and modern *Rome*; and, at the same time, is far above receiving a pecuniary gratification. The Abbé, from an early attachment to the Chevalier and his family, preserves some political prejudices, which certainly have misled him. I shall endeavour to tell you his story; and I do not betray private conversation; for every one here knows it. He says, that, finding the Pretender deserted by the Court of *Rome*, he was cautious enough to ask the Secretary of State, whether he should give umbrage to the Pope, if he paid his visits to him in the character of Count *Douglas*, (the name which the Pretender assumed when he came to *Rome*;) for that he was under such obligations to his Holiness, that he would sacrifice any pleasure, or any duty, rather than give him the least offence. The Secretary assured him, he might continue to pay his respects in that manner, without the least exception. In the course of his visits, it was mentioned to him, that the Pretender took it very ill, of the Superior of the *Scotch* College, that he had neglected him.

The

The Abbé spoke of it to the Superior, who declared, he had been at the Pretender's palace to pay his devoirs, and, hearing nothing since, he supposed, as he was neither received then, nor invited afterwards, that his visit was not acceptable: Presently after this, the Abbé received an anonymous letter, praying him to desire the Superiors of these Colleges to read Mass before the Pretender as to a King: He did so; and, when they signified that they could not dare to contravene the Pope's ordinance, he was zealous enough to recommend some *Franciscans*, who had already performed the ceremony, without having been reprimanded; this was complied with; so that you see he was the great mover. The Pope has ordered him never to come, either alone, or in company, to his palace, and has suspended his appointments*. The Abbé has an infinite number of friends, and the Pope's nephews are his intercessors. He says, in mitigation of his behaviour, that he was at the funeral oration of the late Chevalier, and four Cardinals were present, when

* In a few days his appointments were restored, and in a few weeks he was, as I am informed, received again at *Monte Cavallo*, the Pope's palace.

the preacher, in deploring the loss of *James* the Third, said, "That Heaven, however, had been pleased to give us a full compensation, in the person of his eldest son, *Charles* the Third, King of *Great Britain*, *France*, and *Ireland*, &c. &c." Now, said the Abbé, in his defence, when he was examined; "as this was connived at, he thought the Prince might have been innocently indulged with this poor gratification;" but one of the Cardinals answered this plea, by saying, the one transaction (at the funeral) was done in private, and by obscure persons; the other in the face of day; and that the occasions were of a different nature.

You will conclude, from this long account, that, for the future, the *Stuarts* will be a disagreeable weight on the Pope's shoulders, and that if the Pretender have the least spirit of a man in him, he will bid adieu to *Rome*, and rather take sanctuary in *Constantinople*, amongst *Mahometans*, than remain in a city amongst Papists, for whose tenets his family have forfeited three such glorious kingdoms.

I am, Sir, &c.

LETTER XLV.

FLORENCE, *April* 20, 1766.

SIR,

WE arrived here laft night, after a journey of four days from *Rome*, and found much more agreeable accommodations than we experienced either on the road to *Rome* from *Venice*, or to *Naples* from *Rome*; indeed, to do juftice to the inns, we met with fo much cleanlinefs, and fuch good beds, that we found ourfelves moft agreeably difappointed in thefe articles; and what has added, beyond all expectation, to our pleafure, is the coolnefs of the feafon, which, with all its other advantages, has ftill confined the fleas, the buggs, and the gnats, to their winter-quarters.

It is a melancholy profpect you have always before your eyes, in travelling from *Rome* to the dominions of the Grand Duke, there being very few places where you are not within the diftance of half a mile, or a mile at moft, of dreary barren mountains; no villages, no cottages betwixt the great towns;

towns; and the few people you meet with, carrying the ſtrongeſt marks of poverty and wretchedneſs in their faces and garb. This I diſcovered to be the caſe likewiſe in the rout from *Rome* to *Naples*; yet, were there a proper civil police in theſe countries, the country itſelf is of a nature to enrich its inhabitants; for the ſoil of the vallies is fertile, and would yield abundantly, with a moderate cultivation; and, perhaps, thoſe mountains, which now produce nothing, might, by induſtry and art, be forced to recompence, in ſome degree, the labours of the plowman. At preſent, the Eccleſiaſtical State, and even the kingdom of *Naples*, are either ſterile mountains, or luxuriant vales, as the people are either beggars or nobility.

As uncultivated as many of theſe provinces lie, and as depopulated as we ſee them, compared with antient times, neverthelefs, in every town you paſs through, the men ſtand idling in the ſtreets, and have no occupation; if you upbraid a beggar with his idleneſs, he anſwers, that he cannot find work; and his plea is partly true; for, as they have not the ſpirit of commerce amongſt them, they only think of tilling ſo much ground as will barely

barely subsist the country; and you would wonder to see how little employment there is for artificers of every kind ; so that, in short, the poor have no recourse but to the plough, which can occupy but small numbers, where it is a fashion to live, according to our *English* phrase, *from hand to mouth*. Knowing what I have here related, one cannot be surprized that a scarcity of bread is so common an event in these kingdoms, where no provision is made against such a possibility, by growing more corn than can be consumed, when the year is plentiful. Droughts and tedious rains, both of them common in these climates, ruin a harvest, and then the poor people starve, as they did last year in the Ecclesiastical State, and the year before through the whole territory of *Naples*. Nevertheless, these severe afflictions are not, and, in the nature of things, cannot be a useful lesson to the farmer, unless the Government step in to his aid ; for, as he cannot export any superfluity, it must remain on his hands, and spoil, which will always be an obstacle to plenty ; and both States are so far from adopting our principle of encouraging agriculture, by granting a bounty on the exportation of corn, that they

lay

lay a duty on all exported corn; so little are they convinced of the utility of that police, and so wedded to the ancient opinion of preventing the dearness of bread, by keeping the whole growth at home.

Another great discouragement to agriculture, is the assize put on the price of corn by the Government; however thin the crop be, the farmer is obliged to sell it at that price; this is designed as a relief to the poor, but ultimately is an injury: Corn, like every other merchandize, should find its own fair value, though monopolies are to be discouraged; and, if the farmer be not allowed the same advantages with his commodity, that every other merchant has in his dealings, he will never push to lay in a large stock, or, in other words, will be afraid to till much ground.

Some years since, there was such an amazing harvest through the whole kingdom of *Naples*, that they had upon their hands a quantity to the amount of two or three hundred thousand pounds in value, which they could not consume. There was, at that time, an application made for the exemption of the duty on exportation, without which the merchant could not find his account in sending

it

it abroad; and, though the minister was informed by several, and, among the rest, by an old *Neapolitan* Gentleman of my acquaintance, that the revenue would certainly feel the good effects of so much money brought into the country, as fully as in the shape of a duty on the export, he was deaf to all their reasonings, and would not establish so dangerous a precedent, as he thought it; the consequence was, that the corn grew mouldy, and perished, the next harvest failed, and a dreadful dearth ensued.

Betwixt *Viterbo* and *Radicofani*, lies the town of *Bolsena*, almost in ruins. This place is famous for having given occasion to Pope *Urban* IV. in the fourteenth century, to establish the grand solemnity of the *Fête de Dieu*. It seems that in those days, a priest of *Bolsena* having some doubts concerning the real presence in the Eucharist, God was pleased, they say, to make the wafer bleed when he broke it. You may imagine such a miracle, wrought under his own hands and eyes, could not fail to convince the unbelieving Priest. This miracle is the subject of a fine picture in the Vatican, by *Raphael*.

Upon our entrance into *Tuscany*, we were surprized at the remarkable change in the appearance both of the country and the people. The whole face of *Tuscany* is covered with farm-houses and cottages, an object very rare in the Pope's, or the King of *Naples*'s dominions; but the cottages here, and, indeed, through all *Italy*, are not, as in *France* and *England*, thatched huts, with walls of mud; they are all built of stone or brick, and, to outward appearance, should contain richer inhabitants than in fact they do. The peasantry, in the Grand Duke's dominions, are much handsomer than in the more southern latitudes, look florid, lively, and contented; besides that, they are infinitely better, and more smartly dressed. I am not yet clear to what cause this seeming opulence is to be imputed; whether the genius of the country be more disposed to industry than that of some other parts of *Italy*, or whether the soil itself be more grateful, and the peasant's wages higher; or, possibly, whether the habit of dressing neatly may not be derived from the time of the *Medicis* family, when the country round *Florence* was notoriously the richest spot of ground in *Europe*, and the people of every rank
were

were much more at their eafe than any other fubjects in this part of the globe: I believe, however, from what I am able to learn, that the peafantry here is laborious, and that the land is alfo better cultivated than either in the dominions of his Holinefs, or of the King of the two *Sicilies*...

A ftriking circumftance, though a trivial one, offers itfelf on firft entering the Grand Duke's territories; I mean the ingenious method of figuring their mile-ftones, which I could wifh were imitated in *England*, as time and weather have a tendency to obliterate the figures cut in coarfe ftone, and, what is worfe, as idle boys, in all the world, are apt to make it an amufement to deface the figures of mile-ftones, and deftroy, by that practice, the very ufe of them; the *Florentines*, therefore, let into the figures a fmall flip, or bar of iron, which is faftened with folder, in the ufual manner plumbers fix iron in ftone; by this means the figures on the ftones remain legible almoft for ever, (or, at leaft, would do fo, if the iron were painted black once in two or three years) and the difficulty of breaking them to pieces difcourages the attempt.

In our way to *Florence*, we paſſed through *Sienna*, the town which gave name to the celebrated *Seneſino*; as I had always heard he finiſhed his days very comfortably in his native place, and had built a beautiful palace with the thouſands he had acquired in *England*, one of my firſt enquiries was after his hiſtory and his houſe, which we viſited with a deſign to take only a view of its outſide; but the eagerneſs with which I ſurveyed it, and the appearance of foreigners, ſoon brought the Lady of the houſe to the window, and her politeneſs, together with a good-natured officious forwardneſs in the ſervant who attended me, produced an invitation in leſs than half a minute. She proved to be the wife of *Seneſino*'s eldeſt nephew, and principal heir; a very fine, beautiful, affable woman, and was more rejoiced to ſee us than you can readily imagine, from the grateful ſenſe ſhe entertained of the favours her uncle had received at the hands of the *Engliſh* nation. The houſe is really handſome, but not ſo gaudy and expenſive as to reflect on the modeſty of the owner: Some of the rooms are furniſhed entirely with *Engliſh* furniture, an indication that he had ſome prejudices in favour of

En-

LETTER XLV.

England, as the freight and carriage muſt have been expenſive. It ſtands upon the moſt pleaſant ſpot of ground in the city, and is very gay, becauſe it is the *Corſo,* the place where the gentry take an airing in their coaches. *Seneſino* gave his eldeſt nephew about ten thouſand pounds, and to three or four other nephews, and their ſons, two thouſand five hundred pounds each, a conſiderable fortune at *Sienna,* but not an enormous one.

It is impoſſible for any man, a little acquainted with hiſtory, not to beſtow a ſigh on this once celebrated city and republick, which, when it flouriſhed, ſmall as it was, by the renown of its arms and its arts, made no deſpicable figure in *Europe*; and, in thoſe days (three or four hundred years ſince) contained within its walls ninety or one hundred thouſand inhabitants, where now there are, at moſt, twelve or fourteen thouſand. A plague greatly depopulated it; but the loſs of its liberty proved the incurable wound, which has continued to drain and waſte its ſtrength. The Cathedral is a very curious Gothic ſtructure; the *Sienneſe* call it a fine one, and believe, if it were at *Rome,* it would ſtand in honour next to St *Peter*'s, but I queſtion whether

ther it be not more whimsical than fine: To the best of my memory, the Minster at *York*, though consisting of stone and white walls only, is a more beautiful design; but this building, both on the inside and out, is entirely marble; and what renders it so remarkable, is, that some blocks are white, and others black; there is a large portion of the building white, but the black is in a very considerable quantity; this variegation, upon the first sight, strikes; but I doubt whether, upon the whole, it will stand the test of criticism.

It happened that the very evening of the day I arrived in this city, Sir *Horatio Man*, our Envoy, had provided a most elegant *Conversazione* at his house, in honour of a *Neapolitan* Princess, who was on a visit to her friends at *Florence*; by this accident I had the opportunity of seeing the flower of the *Florentine* nobility; otherwise it is a matter hardly worth mentioning, since the *Italian Conversazioni* differ very little from our *London* routs, being composed of card parties and lookers on.

I am, Sir, &c.

LETTER XLVI.

FLORENCE, *April* 28, 1766.

SIR,

THIS city is paved with larger stones than our foot-paths in *London* are, but they are chiselled in such a manner as to prevent the horses sliding, at least with light carriages, and I see no others; the pavement, therefore, is the smoothest and easiest perhaps in the world. The river *Arno* runs through the town, dividing it as the *Thames* does *London* from *Southwark*. Our lodgings overlook the stream, which, like most others in *Italy*, is turbid; it has found, however, many panegyrical writers, though it have two very bad properties for a river, that is, a propensity to overflow its banks after heavy showers, and to be almost dry at other times. I saw an inscription on the walls of a house, about ten feet from the ground, signifying, that, in the year 1557, the river overflowed the city, to the height of that inscription; there was likewise another in 1761, to the height of two feet in the streets. These inundations happen very often, and, though not to the degree

gree I have described, yet sufficiently to cause much desolation. A short history of the rivers, or, rather, torrents of *Italy*, their frequent emptiness, and their frequent overflowings, would give a man the highest relish for Sir *John Denham*'s few lines in praise of our *Thames*.

I saunter, now and then, in the suburbs, amongst the poor, and not without finding matter of contemplation. I am very well informed, that a woman here, though she have no children and family to take care of, and employ her time, with the utmost diligence, cannot earn above two-pence halfpenny a day by spinning, the usual occupation of the poor; yet, compare either their habitations, or their children, with those of the inhabitants of the skirts of *London*, and you will blush for the misery and dissoluteness of our country-folks. It would be wonderful, however, that the poor could subsist on such small wages, if we did not know, that mere bread alone, and that very coarse, is their principal object of expence. They talk much here of their present wretchedness, the last year having neither produced corn nor wine equal to their home consumption; and, what is worse, (not being

ing a temporary evil, which might be redressed, perhaps, the enfuing year) their manufactures have decayed fo much, that the induftrious cannot always find work: They fay, that, a few years fince, they exported vaft quantities of wrought filks to *England*; now they fend few, or none; nay, that the *Englifh* have gained fo much upon them, in the art of weaving, that they find a profit in importing *Englifh* filk manufactures, particularly filk ftockings, by reafon of their durablenefs. It is true, the prime coft is above one third more than you pay for the fame commodity in *Italy*, but, if it laft twice the time, you know it anfwers. A man fhould come abroad, either to raife his opinion of his country, or his countrymen. I was much pleafed, the other day, to hear an *Englifhman*, who has lived abroad above thirty years, burft into an unfeigned exclamation, upon being fhewn one of the newly invented cork fcrews, *Well!* faid he, *thefe* Englifhmen *are the moft ingenious creatures in the world!*

I have almoft infenfibly quitted my fubject in relation to the poor; but I intended to make a reflection, that, when the populace do not give themfelves up to fpirituous liquors,

quors, they make some shift to scramble through life tolerably well, as may be seen at *Florence*. I am aware that the richest cities will always swarm, for that very reason, with the most indigent poor, so long as men are men; for, since many will be idle, they will, consequently, be, in proportion, more wretched, as the means of subsistence is expensive; and necessaries will grow dearer, as riches multiply: Nevertheless, as brown bread is still cheaper in *England* than elsewhere, I cannot but impute it to pride and idleness, that the greater part of our poor, in and about *London*, are ever in want. The lower people in *Italy* who have bread enough, spend more than you would believe in wine, but neither their abilities, nor the example of their betters, lead them into drunkenness: They have a great notion that it is wholesome, and they give it to their children at the breast. Sir —, and some of the nobles, allow their men servants seven or eight shillings a month for wine, rather than furnish them with it, and, he tells me, they always spend it; for I had figured to myself, that a sober saving man would have drank water, and put the money

in

LETTER XLVI.

in his pocket; but, he says, that examples of that kind are very rare, and almost unknown.

In all the great cities of *Italy*, several shops are shut up, from twelve to half an hour after one, or longer, so sacred is the ceremony of dining; but, indeed, the languor of trade in *Italy* is surprising, and the inactivity of the shopkeepers very often borders upon rudeness. Were commerce more brisk, and were there more rivalship amongst the traders, they would not then lie under the odious imputation that they now do, of sharping, not only foreigners, but their countrymen also, if they can. In *Paris* and *London*, where there is an infinite resort of customers, the tradesman is jealous of his character, and is proud of selling as cheap as his neighbours; he knows, that a small profit on a great number of articles, amounts to one gross sum, and that he shall be detected and deserted, if he impose enormously; on these accounts, he seldom demands much more than he means to accept; whereas in *Italy*, the shopkeeper having but few customers, often asks three, four, and even five times more than the value of the commodity: This fact is so notorious, that strangers are afraid to purchase any thing, except mere

Q   necesneceffaries; and I know by myfelf and my friends, that were trade on the footing here, which it is in *France* and *England*, foreigners would leave more money than they now do in *Italy*. As I have hinted how much the *Italians* make it a point to be undifturbed at dinner, I muft not omit to tell you, that fervants infift on this privilege to a degree truly ridiculous. An *Englifh* Gentleman, not apprifed of the cuftom, upon his firft arrival in *Italy*, poffibly calls his fervant, when the man is juft fat down to dine; but if he call twenty times, he receives no other anfwer, than that he is at dinner *(a Tavola Signore,)* which every *Italian* fervant fuppofes is a fufficient reafon that his mafter fhould wait, though the bufinefs be ever fo preffing. In a fhort time I fubmitted to this fafhion, and at prefent I do not prefume to call up one of our fervants at the hour of dining.

I am much pleafed with the contrivance ufed in the great hofpital here, to avoid bugs; it is no other than a plain bedftead of iron, made fo fimple, that there is not a crevice where a bug can conceal itfelf. I remember, that there have been attempts of this kind made in *England*, but they have proved ineffectual,

LETTER XLVI.

fectual, because they fastened ticking to the frame, with oilet-holes, and cording, which afforded some harbour to these animals. In this hospital they only lay across the frame about four or five boards, a little longer than the width of the frame, and about a foot broad, upon which they lay the bedding; these are moveable, and, if necessary, may be brushed when the bed is made, as easily, and in as short a time, as a man brushes his hat. In the hospitals at *London*, bugs are frequently a greater evil to the patient, than the malady for which he seeks an hospital; and, could I have interest enough with the governors, to bring about an imitation of this frame, I should be exceedingly rejoiced in the comfort it will afford to so many thousands of miserable wretches, that are tormented sometimes even to death, by these nauseous vermin.

I am, Sir, &c.

LETTER XLVII.

FLORENCE, *May* 2, 1766.

SIR,

THERE is but one theatre open at *Florence*, juft at this juncture, and there is feldom more than one at a time, except in the feafon of the Carnival, when the rage of frequenting fpectacles is fuch in *Italy*, that, in this fmall city, the people fill fix or feven houfes every night; but, in fhort, as if it were an act of devotion, every body makes a point of going; whereas in *France*, the madnefs of a carnival is, in a manner, unknown. There are, however, at *Florence*, but three confiderable theatres, one very large, and two of about the dimenfions of that in *Drury-lane*. The large one is dedicated to the ferious Opera, the other two to comedy and burlettas. Upon a calculation, I find, that, though the extent of the houfe, now open, be equal to that of *Drury-lane*, it does not contain near the number of people, from the nature of its form, it having no galleries, but confifting merely of boxes and pit. The pit I apprehend to be twice as big as ours,

LETTER XLVII.

ours, but the boxes must be incommodiously crammed to receive seven hundred people; whereas, if I remember rightly, our two galleries alone will hold near a thousand. The comedy they exhibit here is very low indeed, by no means exceeding what is called, in *England*, a droll, and what would be very tiresome to an *Englishman*, but for the pleasure there is in novelty. To give you some idea of the small progress of the drama through all *Italy*, I need only repeat, that I have never yet seen there one play consisting of five acts; and that the joy it affords arises from mistaking one word for another, blunders, indelicate jokes, &c. At *Paris*, *Harlequin* is allowed some freedoms, which, I believe, would hardly be suffered in a *London* theatre (however *Frenchmen* may value themselves on the elegance of their taste,) but then the *Parisians* have the resource of another theatre, where both tragedy and comedy may be said to flourish almost to perfection; whereas *Harlequin* and the other *Italian* characters of *Punch*, *Don Fastidio*, *Pantaloon*, &c. are, in a manner, the only characters you see on the stages of this country. The *Harlequin* of this theatre is very popular, and, what you will be surprized at, very rich, though the salary paid both to him and his wife be but seventy-five pounds a year sterling; but, to solve the riddle, you must know, that the *Harlequin* is a tradesman, and, perhaps, may have as much merit in that department, as in his black face and party-coloured suit; however it be, he is a great favourite, and his shop is much frequented: I have been his customer for no other reason, in preference, but the singularity of the tradesman: His journeyman, another actor, is the fine Gentleman of the *Florentine* Stage. Mr *Addison*, and Sir *William Temple*, I believe, have both spoken with great applause of the *Dutch* theatres, because the company of comedians was said to be composed of artificers, who, after their day's labour, recreated themselves and the publick, with their dramatick exhibitions, not making the profession, as in other kingdoms, an idle calling: But, with submission to such great men, I should imagine, were the practice general, it would spoil both the tradesman and the actor; and these sober comedians would frequently become bankrupts.

We

We have much more pleasure at their burletta operas, than at their comedies, though they have not in their company any singer or actor of very distinguished talents; but, upon the whole, it does very well, and passes off the evening pleasantly. The church keeps a strict hand over *Tuscany*, as well as the other states of *Italy*. On the page of the Opera-book, where, in *England*, the argument is usually printed off, you have here, in capital letters, a *Protesta*. This protest is a declaration, that though the writer of the drama has made use of the words *God, Gods, Deities, &c.* he means no offence to the church, but that in conformity to the Mythology of the Antients, he has been obliged to introduce those fables and those phrases.

I never trouble you with descriptions of churches and palaces, but, rather, with the customs and manners of the people I visit; yet I cannot forbear mentioning the ducal palace at *Florence*, which has, by far, the most noble range of rooms I ever beheld: I should not, however, have thought this circumstance worth a paragraph in my letter, but for this particular, that it was built by one *Pitti*, a private man, before the establishment of the *Medici* family, into whose hands it immediately fell; yet, in spite of their great reputation and magnificence, through a long course of years it still retains the name of its first owner, and is called the *Pitti* palace to this hour. I own to you, I look with admiration on this monument of *Tuscan* taste and grandeur, and cannot but reflect with astonishment on the low ebb of commerce, and the fine arts, in other states of *Europe*, when they flourished with so much vigour in this dutchy.

The gardens are esteemed fine by the *Italians*, but, in the eyes of an *Englishman*, they are execrable; undoubtedly our taste in gardening is much more elegant than that of the *Italians*; besides, as they cannot have either green grass or fine gravel, they want some of the proper materials to render a garden perfectly beautiful; but, what is unpardonable and absurd, amongst a thousand other defects in their laying out a garden, is, their contrivance to calculate them for winter when nobody walks, and not for summer when gardens are agreeable. This absurdity is, the prodigious number of large trees, all of the ever-green kind, with which their gardens abound; it is true, they afford a shade; but of so dismal a hue as is hardly to be

be imagined; and, at the times they want shade, trees of a beautiful verdure would be stocked with leaves: Certainly this vice will be reformed as their taste improves. If they adapt their gardens to the winter, they almost as preposterously build their houses for the summer only, notwithstanding the rigour of the winter in this mountainous country. It is hardly thirty years ago, that, except kitchen chimneys, there were scarcely any, not only in *Naples*, but even in the Northern latitude of *Venice*. Antiquity renders every custom venerable, and almost sacred; but still you would wonder to see how prejudiced the *Italians* are against the introduction of chimneys; they have an idea that they must be unwholsome, so little do they understand the nature of a ventilator, and that a thorough draught must purify the air we breathe. It happened that my chimney at *Naples* took fire, being ill built, and having never been swept since it was erected (about three or four years;) this accident so alarmed the landlord, that he demurred whether he should not turn a Gentleman who lodged over my head, out of his apartments, because he refused to pull down his chimney on this occasion. The Gentleman is, certainly, one of the best tenants in
Naples,

Naples, and the landlord's interest at last prevailed over his frights and prejudices; but he lives in a state of unhappiness, that his house should be prostituted to the vile use of chimneys.

Through all *Tuscany* the inhabitants have a guttural pronunciation, which prevails, too, even amongst their gentry, and, sometimes, to a gross degree. I have often heard it said, that the purest *Italian* is spoken at *Sienna*; but I am very well persuaded, that were a child sent there to learn the language, he would acquire this imperfection of speech. One of the most ingenious men I have seen in *Italy*, is a *Siennese*, and has the guttural pronunciation to the greatest excess; however, he is so little conscious of it, that he frequently asserts the charge against *Tuscany* is groundless and scandalous; the assertion seldom fails to make us smile, as he cannot speak without furnishing a proof of the allegation. I know an *English* Gentleman who has lived here so many years, that he is become as blind as the *Siennese* to this defect of the *Tuscans*, but is now and then so guilty of it himself, as even to speak *English* gutturally, without being in the least sensible of it. It is curious to observe
how

how many ages the same virtue or the same vice continues to be local. *Dante* complains of this very defect, as general, in his time, and which, probably, had subsisted from time immemorial amongst the people of *Tuscany*. I presume, that in all countries a man may attain the purest language and accent, where the best company resides, which will always be in the metropolis. I should therefore suppose, as *Florence* is exceptionable, that *Rome* (if it were possible to avoid countrymen) is the place where a foreigner should go for *Italian*. It is a well known proverb, *Lingua Toscana in Bocca Romana*.—That is to say, *The* Tuscans *write pure* Italian, *the* Romans *pronounce it purely*; but, though that part of the proverb which regards the pronunciation be undoubtedly true, some *Romans* dispute the other.

By what I can foresee, *Florence*, in our judgment, will be preferred to all the other cities in *Italy* as a place of residence; though perhaps we may be partial in our opinions, as accidents contribute to raise or sink the ideas of travellers in their estimation of places; and here we run a risk of being extremely prejudiced, as the polite and courteous behaviour of Sir *Horatio Man* to all his coun-

countrymen, must have made our stay very agreeable, had the place and the people been ever so exceptionable and unpleasing.

I am, Sir, &c.

LETTER XLVIII.

FLORENCE, *May* 6, 1766.

SIR,

WHILST I am in *Italy*, I seldom fail to be present every evening at the Theatres, as being the place where, next to good company, a traveller is best enabled to catch the manners of a people. I have, for the first time, seen a comedy here, of five acts; and, what I did not expect to meet with on the *Italian* stage, a Tragedy; it is translated from *Voltaire*'s *Mahomet*, and though Tragedy be so little cultivated in *Italy*, I perceived the audience were more attentive than I ever saw them at any other exhibition; so forcible are the dramatic powers of *Voltaire*, even in the disguise of a translation.

If

LETTER XLVIII.

If a man may dare to pronounce upon the stage and language of a foreign country, I think the *Italian* tragick declamation is far from indifferent in its nature; it appears to me much more sweet and pathetic, I might also venture to say natural, than the declamation of the *French* Tragedians; but I do not see any prospect of the *Italian* stage being raised to the dignity it is susceptible of: There must be a succession of Princes to protect, honour, and reward both poets and players, before such a reformation can be effected; but you will conceive at how low an ebb these liberal arts are at *Florence*, when I tell you the price of the pit is only six-pence *English*.

I have the honour to be much with the Abbé *Nicolini*, who, though he live here, is by birth a *Roman*, and his estate lies in the Pope's dominions; he is uncle to the Prince *Corsini*; he was very well known in *England* during the years 1746-7-8, by his connections with Lord *Chesterfield*, Lord *Bath*, Lord *Melcomb*, and that set of Gentlemen the late Prince of *Wales* was pleased to honour with his esteem and friendship. He speaks *English* almost to perfection, and by virtue of his

par-

particular talents, good sense, and long opportunity of studying our laws and customs, he has attained to such a knowledge of them as, I believe, no foreigner besides could ever pretend to. My conversations with this nobleman on the plan of *English* law, and *English* liberty, has suggested to me a new opinion, that though *England* be not a fashionable object for travellers, as *Italy* and *France* are, yet could a foreigner possess our language to the perfection as some of us do *French* and *Italian*, and, were he a man of so liberal a turn of mind, as to make the system of our laws and liberties his principal pursuit, I think it is the country of the world, where such a man would find the most pleasure, and the most improvement. It is with a fondness bordering on enthusiasm, that the Abbé talks on these subjects, and you will not wonder if he declare, that could he lay aside the partiality for his own country, which Providence has been kindly pleased to plant in the breast of every man, *England* is the kingdom where he would fix his residence.

The Grand Duke I find, upon good authority, to be a young man, of a most benevolent disposition; but the excess of this virtue

tue becomes a vice; his charity leads him to encourage beggars to such a degree that they multiply enormously, and hang in such numbers about his horses and coach, that they obstruct his passage through the streets. This encouragement of beggary will soon corrupt the industrious poor, and I really think that at this instant, I see more beggars in *Florence* than I ever saw, even at *Rome*, where no vagrant is driven out, as they are in every other city of *Italy*, after the third day. I presume his eyes will shortly be opened to this abuse, and that he will lay aside the charitable character, to assume that of the politician; if he do not, the evil will still increase; for idleness is catching, and few will work, who can find a support without working. He has a great ambition to be informed; but I question whether the late Emperor, and the Queen of *Hungary* (his father and mother) were so eager to instruct, as he was to be instructed; at present he is much delighted with experimental philosophy, and, I am told, has a remarkable inclination to chymistry; he is but nineteen, and therefore may become a knowing man if these accounts be true, and he have the good fortune to fall into able hands. His
body

body guard confists of young nobles only; they are about fifty-two in number, and will certainly, in a few weeks, be by far the most magnificent troop in *Europe*. Their new uniform, and horse furniture, will then be ready, and I am told will cost sixty thousand crowns; which divided amongst fifty two, amounts to above a thousand crowns *English* for each man and horse. The army is small; I believe, in the whole dutchy, there are not above five thousand men, which, however, are more than they want, as the security of *Tuscany* depends wholly on its situation, and the interest of her neighbours, that she should be unmolested. Look on the Map, and you will see it surrounded by the Ecclesiastical State, and the Republick of *Lucca*, which must be invaded before an enemy can penetrate into the Dutchy.

The neighbourhood of *Florence* is delightful; the hills round the town, at the distance of two or three miles, form an amphitheatre, where a thousand country houses, built of white stone, beautify the prospect. The fields, and indeed the whole face of *Tuscany*, are in a manner covered with olive-trees; but the olive-tree does not answer the character

LETTER XLVIII.

ter I had conceived of it: The Royal Pfalmift, and fome of the facred writers, fpeak with rapture of the green olive tree, fo that I expected a beautiful green; and I confefs to you, I was wretchedly difappointed to find its hue refemble that of our hedges, when they are covered with duft. The olive-tree may, poffibly, delight in the barren diftrict of *Judæa*, but undoubtedly, will difguft a man accuftomed to *Englifh* verdure.

Madam *Minorbetti*, a woman of diftinction, has, through the means of ―――― ――――, fhewn great civilities to my daughters; I mention her name for having given occafion to one of the moft ridiculous events that has fallen within my knowledge, and which will put to fhame fome of the *Greek* etymologies we are entertained with in the pofthumous works of Dean *Swift*. You may remember, he afferts, for the honour of *Great Britain*, that many of thofe names which we fuppofe to be originally *Greek* are really derived from the *Britifh* language, and, by corruption, have attained the caft of the *Greek* tongue. For example; he fays, "that *Andromache* is a corruption of the *Scotch* name *Andrew Mackey: Archimedes*, of

Hark ye Maids, &c. &c." It seems, that a relation of Madam *Minorbetti*, in the agonies of death, was desirous to have a famous relick in this city, no less than an arm of our Archbishop *Becket*, brought to his bed-side, from a persuasion he should be restored to health, by its miraculous influence: The Monks, in whose possession the arm is, rejected the petition, and pleaded the impossibility of carrying it beyond the precincts of the convent; the relations, on the other hand, urged, that they were descended from the family of the *Beckets*, and, therefore, that such a usage might be dispensed with; the argument was admitted to be good, and the Monks demanded only a proof of the consanguinity, which was demonstrated in the following manner:—" A Bishop, said they, in *England*, is always called *Milor*, (my Lord) which easily, in *Italian*, is corrupted into *Minor*; then *Becket* as easily degenerates into *Betti*; so that *Milor-becket* naturally becomes *Minor-betti*." This notable argument was deemed so valid, that the relick was brought out of the convent to the sick man.—Do not doubt the truth of the fact

LETTER XLVIII.

fact becaufe of its ludicroufnefs; you may depend on every circumſtance of the ſtory.

At all the houſes of the Nobles in *Florence,* you ſee an empty flaſk hanging out, to denote they ſell wine by retail; this cuſtom ſhocks an *Engliſhman,* as a practice very derogatory from their dignity, and he cannot but ſpeak of it with ſurprize. A *Florentine* cooly and ſenſibly anſwers, " Sir, your Duke
" of ——, by the interpoſition of a ſteward,
" ſells a tree for ten ſhillings; our Noble, by
" his porter at the door, ſells ten ſhillings
" worth of wine; but our noble appears no
" more in the ſale of the wine, than your
" Duke of ————, in the ſale of his tree;
" different countries have their different
" modes."—The truth is, that, through all *Italy,* great part of the rent for eſtates, is paid in kind, which, joined with a certain exemption from the impoſt on wine, granted to the nobles in *Florence,* has led them, I believe, into this ſeeming littlenefs.

I was the other night, at a moſt elegant concert, given by the *Lucchefe* Envoy, at his own palace. The faſhion, upon this occaſion, is to calculate the number of people the rooms will hold, and to invite accordingly; but Ladies only are invited. It is computed, that cards sent to twenty-five or twenty-six Ladies, will bring near fourscore Gentlemen; and the number at this assembly answered to that calculation. The great disproportion betwixt the number of Ladies at the *Italian Converzationi*, and the *London* routs, is very striking to an *Englishman*; but the phænomenon admits of an easy solution. No single Ladies, as I have told you before, visit in *Italy*; all who are seen in the world are married women. If a Gentleman here have three sons and three daughters, two of the daughters are most probably in a convent, whilst all the three sons, at least two of them, have nothing else to do, than to frequent the Spectacles and *Converzationi*.

The palace of the *Lucchese* Envoy is very large; so are the palaces of all the Nobles in *Florence*; indeed they are of such an extent, that usually one floor only is occupied at the same time. During the winter, they inhabit the upper apartments; and, during the summer, they reside altogether on the ground-floor; a most agreeable piece of luxury in the Northern Parts of *Italy*, which are so extremely hot, and so extremely cold

in

in the two seasons. House-rent at *Florence* is still cheaper than at *Venice*.

In *Florence*, the generality of Ladies have each of them three Cicesbeos; the first is the Cicesbeo of dignity; the second is the Cicesbeo who picks up the glove, gives the fan, and pulls off, or puts on the cloak, &c. the third Cicesbeo is, by the wags, deemed the substantial Cicesbeo, or Lover.—God knows how these matters go; for, in public, the Ladies behave with so much modesty and decorum, that I should be tempted to treat some of these reports as mere calumny, were not the truth of them so notorious; in fact, the universality of the vice has, in a manner, divested it of the appearance of vice: With us, a woman who is publickly criminal, usually becomes profligate and abandoned; here, almost every woman, of however virtuous a disposition, falls into the general custom, and is equally criminal with the woman of loose principles; so that the distinction of good and bad, I mean chaste and dissolute, is hardly known in *Italy*; in a word, 'tis the mode, the *etiquette*, the *bon ton* of the fine people; and now wives and Cicesbeos hardly give more scandal than wives and husbands, excite as little animadversion when together, and, indeed, exclusive of gallantry, lead as innocent and sober lives.

I shall finish this letter with an extract, taken from a curious survey of the Dutchy of *Tuscany*, made on the accession of the present Grand Duke. It contains an account of the numbers of inhabitants in the several districts of this principality; and is certainly a measure of government, worthy the imitation of every state, as nothing can tend to enlighten an administration, so much, in regard to the real strength of a kingdom, as a thorough knowledge of the numbers of the several classes of the people. This survey is not printed, but as I was allowed the liberty to make what use I pleased of the manuscript, I thought I could not furnish you a more agreeable entertainment, than the sums total of the several classes, which are as follow:

Married men	142699
———— women	143590
Unmarried men	180348
———— women	190874
Boys	128199
Girls	

Girls	119986
Churchmen	3529
Priests	8355
Monks	5548
Hermits	144
Nuns	9349
Protestant men	230
———— women	55
Jews, men	4464
Jews, women	4513
Total	941883

I am, Sir, &c.

LETTER XLIX.

BOLOGNA, *May* 9, 1766.

SIR,

WE are arrived at *Bologna* in two days, after a pleasant, or rather, an amusing journey; for travelling so long a way amongst the barren *Appennines* can hardly be called pleasant. The country, however, for several

several miles, after we left *Florence*, was very agreeable, and still more agreeable for some miles before we reached *Bologna*, as there are no olive trees in the neighbourhood of this last city, but a verdure almost rivalling ours in *England*. It happened to be a week of a remarkable Function, called the Procession of the Rogation (Rogation Week,) when all the communities of the city, walk several days in form, every man with a wax taper in his hand, and every community with a Crucifix, or dying Saviour: The images are of different sizes, from one foot to four feet high, and of different designs; in all of them he is crowned with thorns; but in some, the thorns have not wounded him, in others his face and neck are covered with drops or streams of blood. During the procession, both through the church and streets, there is an accompanyment of martial musick, and tolling of bells. There was such an extraordinary succession of crucifixes, (I think about fifty-four of them) that I was much tired of the sameness of the objects; but at last, the appearance of a *Madona*, which closed the procession, brought me relief. She was painted, as are many others in *Europe*,

by

by St *Luke*, and is much reverenced here, for the number of miracles she has wrought in favour of the *Bolognese*. This ceremony would provoke some Protestants, and furnishes all with strong arguments against Catholick tenets and practices; for, during the appearance of the several figures of *Christ*, the people were so indifferent, that I observed some of them stood with their hats on; but, upon the exhibition of the Blessed Virgin, they not only prostrated themselves on their knees, but, in answer to three bows made by the picture, they, in the attitude of kneeling, bent their heads to the ground three times. At the church-door, there was a kind of Litany pronounced, to the praise of the Blessed Virgin, where the response of the people, for several minutes together, was, *Ora pro nobis*. A moderate Catholick may refine, and plead, that the picture is not an object of worship, but a mere memento of the Virgin; yet, a man who travels through Popish countries, will always believe that the picture itself is honoured; and a Protestant may naturally ask, how it happens, that one *Madona* has more fame and more power than another, if it be only a picture to remind us of the original?

ginal? I could write you a letter every week on the single subject of vulgar religious prejudices, were I to enumerate all those I hear; but I cannot forbear telling you that the common people of *Bologna* believe, that if the *Madona* were not carried in this procession, she, the picture, would descend from her station, and walk through the streets.

At *Rome*, there is a society, who advance money to the poor (upon depositing a pawn) without interest. This design appears useful; but I had not an opportunity of learning whether it be abused, as most other good intentions are. I should not have mentioned it, but that I have seen a like institution at *Bologna*, with this remarkable ancient inscription over the gate of the building where the business is transacted, *This institution was, &c. &c. in order to put an end to the usury practised by the Jews.* The truth is, that in those times the *Jews* were the only factors, or money-lenders in *Europe*; and it is no wonder, that what was a *Jewish* practice, should be held in such detestation by Christians; but, with the times, we see the modes of religion totally alter, and good Bishops now make no scruple to receive five *per cent.* if they can get

get it honestly. A few days since, I bestowed a minute's pensive contemplation on the monument of *Galileo*. I could not but reflect, with sorrow, and some indignation, that the Priests of the same church treated him as a blasphemer, for asserting the *Copernican* system, who now treat the *Hutchinsonians* as fanaticks, for doubting it. I am not to tell you, that poor *Galileo* remained in the prisons of the Inquisitions many years, suffering extreme hardships in his old age there, and was not set at liberty till he retracted his doctrine.

At *Bologna*, as at *Florence*, the Nobles are numerous and poor; indeed, for the same reason; that is to say, because all the children are noble, and because it is a fashion to divide their estates almost equally amongst them: This custom had a very good effect, when it was honourable to be engaged in commerce, as was the case when the trade of *Europe* was in a manner carried on by the Nobles of *Florence*, *Venice* and *Lombardy*: Every son, by this article, improved his fortune, and enriched his country; but the discovery of the passage to the *Indies*, by the *Cape of Good Hope*, putting an end to this

mono-

monopoly, and to the exorbitant gains attending it, commerce, by degrees, became contemptible, as it grew less profitable; and the Nobility, finding no resources beyond their pitiful incomes, became wretched, at least the greater part of them. I have been credibly informed, that a Noble at *Florence*, with five hundred pounds a year, is reputed to be in pretty good circumstances; though there are a few, who have some thousands: But poor as the *Italian* Nobles are, from this circumstance of dividing their estates amongst their sons, they would still be more so, were it a custom for all the sons to marry: But it seems to be a rule established through all *Italy*, that one or two only of them should marry, the others preserving themselves single, with the view that their estates may revert, and by that means support the dignity of their family.

 I should have told you, when I wrote from *Florence*, that the last sixteen years, by an order of the late Emperor, clocks after the *English* manner have been used in *Tuscany*; the lower people still talk of 24 o'clock, and the first and second hour of the night; but, I should suppose, that, in the northern parts of
Italy,

Italy, this inconvenient method of counting the hours, will be abolished in a few years; for at *Parma*, and *Placentia* also, the *Engilsh* method gains ground.

ALEXANDRIA, *May* 12, 1766.

THE country from *Bologna* to this place is a delightful, fertile plain, and the accommodations so much better than those we meet with on the road to *Rome*, by the way of *Loretto*, that I desire you will make the distinction betwixt my journey thither, and my return, whenever you give a character of *Italy* from my letters.

Walking in the gardens of the palace at *Parma*, I had the good fortune to see the young Duke; he is the most manly youth I ever beheld, and has a great reputation. The King of *France*, his grandfather, appointed him able preceptors, and, it is said, they have cultivated his genius in a very extraordinary manner: It is certain that he has had great advantages, and the example of his own father, the late Don *Philip*, was no small one, who, undoubtedly, was a virtuous Prince. He is but little more than fifteen years of age: I was

close

close to him long enough to pronounce, that his demeanor is courteous and elegant.

Here, as in most parts of *Italy*, the size of the palace, now building, is too gigantic for the court, and the expence of it too great for the treasury; so it remains, and will for ever remain, half finished. The garden is likewise in a rude condition. A certain Gentleman, of great figure in the world, told a friend of mine, that, some years since, having had the honour to dine with Don *Philip*, in the course of conversation, he gave an opinion, that were the garden his, he would do so and so.—*Aye*, said the Duke, *and were I you, Sir, I would do just the same thing; but, Sir,* added he, *I have not a shilling to do it; my brother, the King of* Spain, *has stript my palaces, has emptied my gallery, and believe me, my pockets are as empty as my gallery.*—The truth of part of this assertion is very notorious; for many of the curious pictures and statues were sent from *Parma* to *Naples* and *Spain*.

TURIN, *May* 14, 1766.

WE are arrived at *Turin*; but the journey from *Alexandria* has been unpleasant; one night's rain has made the road almost impaffable, fo muddy and fo clayey is the foil. I fhould conclude, therefore, that, in winter, it is more advifeable to travel from *Placentia* to *Turin* by the way of *Milan*, though it be a little farther than by the road of *Alexandria*. The whole country is extremely fertile, and to a degree, that it may be truly faid, there is not an acre of barren ground through all the tract of *Lombardy* which we have paffed. The earth produces three crops at once, wine, filk, and corn. The mulberry-trees fupport the vines, and the corn grows in the intervals betwixt the trees. It is certainly an inftance of extraordinary plenty; but probably, either of the three products would be more perfect in their kind, if the foil were appropriated to one or two of them only. From ten miles beyond *Bologna*, to this place, I did not fee an olive tree; fo that the verdure is much more beautiful than in *Tufcany*.

I am, Sir, &c.

LETTER L.

TURIN, *May* 18, 1766.

SIR,

I POSTPONED giving you any account of *Turin* till my return, hoping I should have been able to entertain you much more agreeably, by a second visit to this city; but I find, upon examination, that the descriptions I have already sent you of *Italian* customs and manners, anticipate almost every thing I had to say upon that subject in relation to *Turin*. What few peculiarities I have observed concerning both the place and the people, I shall, however, make the subject of two or three letters.

The apartments of the palace are much more magnificent than is to be expected from its outward appearance; and, perhaps, were they as large as those at *Versailles*, might vie with them in elegance and furniture: They are certainly a beautiful range of rooms, and are one amongst the very few instances where the real merit exceeds the popular character. His Majesty, the Duke of *Savoy*, and the younger son the Duke of *Chablais* are all

much

much beloved; but the Duke of *Savoy*, the heir apparent, is almost adored by the people. The King, through the course of a long reign, has supported such a reputation for policy, assiduity, and faithfulness to his engagements, that you will not charge me with an affectation of wisdom, if I assert, that the government of this country is carried on with more spirit, and less corruption, than that of any other in *Italy*, or, perhaps, in *Europe*.

His Majesty is certainly one of the most regular men in the world; indeed his life is so regular that it is almost mechanical. He gives audience from six to eleven every morning; goes to Mass about twenty minutes before twelve; dines at half an hour after twelve; generally takes an afternoon's airing; then plays one or two hours in the nursery with his grand-children; and sups so exactly at ten, that they told me, he leaves the Opera sometimes a few minutes before it is finished, if it exceed ever so little the hour of ten. His virtue is so rigid, that the gallantry of the Cicesbeos gives him much offence; and he is so scandalized at this fashion, that he discountenances it to the utmost of his power; but I perceive no human power can destroy a mode so well established, and so flattering to our depravity; for both at the Corso and the Spectacles, the ladies still appear with their Cicesbeos, in defiance of the royal displeasure.

The Airing or Corso in these countries is always understood to be in coaches: The gentry never walk, as the *French* Ladies do in the *Thuilleries*, and the *English* in St *James*'s-*Park*; but the Corso in coaches is the first and predominant pursuit, to which all others are subservient. Thus all over *Italy* the hours of opening the Spectacles wait on the length of the days; that is, in the longest days, the Corso finishes a little before eight o'clock, and then the theatres open; but when the days are shorter, the theatres open sooner; so that in winter the Spectacles begin betwixt five and six; but, in the very hot nights of the summer, the *Corso*, in some cities of *Italy*, continues almost till morning, when the *Italians* are as riotous as their sobriety admits of, regaling themselves, according to their fashion, with ices, sweet-meats, and lemonades.

There are two theatres at *Turin*; the one for the serious Opera, almost as large and magnificent as that at *Naples*; the second, a smaller, for the three other kinds of Spectacles,

cles, namely, the *Comedie Françoise*, the *Comedie Italienne*, and the *Opera Comique*. These four exhibitions succeed each other in the four different seasons of the year; but the King and Family never frequent any but the Grand Opera. I do not learn that his Majesty lays himself under this restraint from any religious exception to a play-house, but merely because it is the etiquette of the court. Should the Royal Family break through this ridiculous form, it would certainly tend to improve their stage, and render the Spectacles more brilliant; but they have a custom here which will always preserve elegance and decorum in their operas. There is a society of forty Gentlemen, answerable for every expence whatsoever, *viz.* the salaries of the actors and the orchestra, the purchase of the scenery, the dresses, *&c. &c.* so that the performers are sure of their pay, though the opera should not succeed. It is not so with regard to the *Italian* and *French* Comedians, those two companies taking the chance of good and bad houses.

In my walks, not far from the city, I accidentally saw a mill for grinding corn, the mechanism of which is very remarkable;

perhaps,

perhaps there may be some of the same kind in *England*; but, as probably you never saw such a one, I will endeavour to give you some idea of it. It is a contrivance to avail themselves of the benefit of every ounce of water in the river. In the generality of mills, however large the body of water be, it is seldom applied, as I apprehend, to the turning of more than two or three wheels; in this instance, if I remember rightly, there are towards twenty. The river which supplies the mill, I guess, by my steps, to be about thirty-six feet wide; it is very rapid, and, by means of a flood-gate, rises to a great height, and falls in large quantities over the flood-gate, down a considerable depth, into several troughs placed on the other side, and is conveyed by them into the bed of the river. The troughs are about two or three feet diameter, and are of different lengths, having, at their extremities, a wheel of such a size, as the weight of water in the trough can turn with a sufficient velocity. The same mechanism is practised by a body of water which falls from the side of the river into another river below it; but as words only will hardly make you comprehend the design, I have annexed a drawing, which,

LETTER L. 273

which, perhaps, may illuftrate what I have meant to explain.

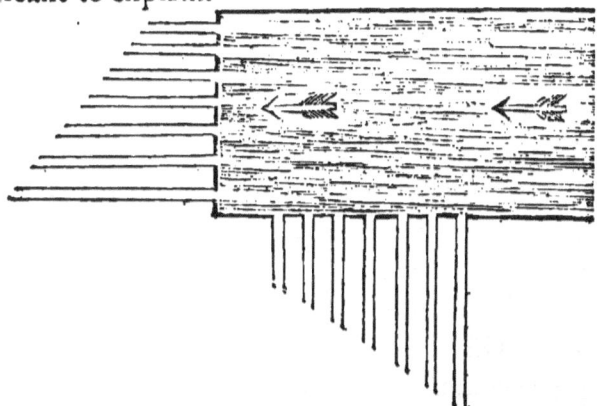

In this figure you fee, at a glance, a number of troughs, which I have fuppofed fourteen, though I think there are more. Imagine a wheel under the extremity of each trough, and you will conceive, from their oblique termination, that there is a fufficient fpace for feven wheels, &c. It is this multiplicity of wheels which conftitutes the ingenioufnefs of the device, and renders the mill equal in powers to two or three mills, becaufe the weight of every drop of water is employed to a good purpofe, none of it falling fuperfluoufly on any of the wheels.

I am, Sir, &c.

LETTER LI.

Turin, *May* 19, 1766.

SIR,

WHILST I am at *Turin*, I go every day to the King's antichamber, to see him and his Court pass to chapel, and as constantly wait on them through the whole service: If merely attending on public worship be a work of merit, I may vaunt with the Pharisee in the Gospel, of my great desert. You will wonder to hear so much of my perseverance in the pursuit of these religious ceremonies; but, as the folly I am enquiring after is infinite, were I to live here for ever, the search would likewise be endless. The good old King, in his latter days, gives himself up entirely to devotion; the rest of the family too are exceedingly devout: The church, therefore, is triumphant at *Turin*, and the chief splendor of this city is to be found in the King's chapel. He has a choice Orchestra, at the head of which are *Pugnani*, and the two *Bisoucis*. He seldom prays to God, but as *Nebuchadnezzar* prayed to his God, with the sound of the sackbut, the psalter,

ter, and all kinds of mufical inftruments. Certainly, if a gilded church be an honour to the Deity, he is much more honoured in *Italy* than in *England*, and the Catholic Religion, if I may ufe the expreffion, is much more flattering to him than our plain home-fpun form of prayer.

On *Saturday* laft, the whole mafs was performed in the pantomime manner, the prieft not pronouncing one word aloud, but only accompanying the mufick through the whole office, with a thoufand unintelligible geftures. The day following being *Whitfunday*, there was a high mafs, which continued exactly fifty minutes, and was celebrated both by mufick, and by chanting. The tricks played by the priefts, and their attendants, during the celebration, are fo whimfical, that, were I capable of defcribing them, you would imagine I had fat down to invent raillery, farcafm, and carricature. To give you fome idea of one part: Imagine four young men in fcarlet banyans, and white nightrails, walking half the time of the fervice before the altar; one moment bowing like the judges in *Bays*'s dance, to the king, the next moment to the altar, and, prefently after, to the ground, ringing the changes in this manner for fifty minutes: then each of them has a large lighted taper, which, for a certain length of time, they carry horizontally, walking solemnly one after another, with the same care as you would step along a narrow deal board, without touching the cracks of the floor: After this proceffion they bend both knees towards the ground, but not fo far as to touch the ground, juft in the method you have feen dancers on the flack rope, but fomething more deliberately; after this, they raife themfelves from that uneafy pofture, to an erect fituation, but with fo circumfpect and gradual a motion, that they tremble and totter, not without fome rifk of falling; when the genuflexion and elevation are finifhed, or, rather, during the operation, the tapers are thrown into various pofitions, as a foldier would exercife with a pique or a mufket. How the fertile and foolifh brain of man could invent all this foppery and nonfenfe is wonderful; but it would, perhaps, be curious, could we come at the hiftory of its origin, and on what pretence thefe feveral practices were introduced. I am afraid to go on with my defcription, becaufe I feel myfelf myself unequal to the ridiculousness, and, indeed, lest I should forfeit the character of veracity, by telling truths so very like falshoods; but I must not omit to mention, that, at a certain moment, (I think the instant after the elevation of the Host) the two Priests who officiate at the altar, embrace and kiss other priests who sit on the bench near the altar, with a solemnity and grimace truly ludicrous. I confess it is seldom pardonable, to deride the ceremonies of any religion sincerely professed by its followers; but, when the ceremonies of a religion are farcical, and so palpably the instruments of oppression and tyranny, by which the common sense and civil rights of the world are enslaved to a proud priesthood, it were virtue to laugh till men grew ashamed of their folly.

Pugnani is in the highest reputation for his proficiency on the violin, and, in the opinion of the *Italians*, and even the *English* at *Turin*, is superior to *Giardini*. It has been my good fortune to hear him to the greatest advantage; but, if I may hazard my sentiments on this delicate point, though I must tell you, I am singular in my judgment, I prefer *Giardini*, and esteem him a much
more

more agreeable performer than *Pugnani*. It is said, that *Pugnani* draws out a louder tone from the upper part of the fiddle, than *Giardini* does; and this, it must be granted, is his forte; but, with submission to *Italian* ears, mine were a little shocked in several parts of his solo. I wished he had been a little more sweet, though he had been less forte; and, from this example of so excellent a performer, it may be suspected that a very short string, will not admit of a sweet tone beyond such a degree of loudness. His taste and elegance I thought by no means comparable to *Giardini*'s; but, perhaps, I may have been mistaken in all my criticisms; however, I am persuaded, though my judgment may be false, that it does not spring from a want of feeling; for the *Bisoucis*, both of them, (the hautbois and the bassoon) gave me the pleasure I expected from their fame, who, though they are extremely old, have still the same powers as formerly. Most probably *Pugnani* will find his way to *England* some time or another; but, at present, I am told the King will not suffer it; for, though his Majesty have no relish for music, he will have the best hands he can procure for divine service. I suppose, were a plain Christian to ask, why all this noise and parade in divine worship? why all these drums, trumpets, and clangor? Are not a good life, a devout heart, and a sober prayer, the most pleasing offering that can be made to the Deity; the men with shaved heads, holy water, sweet burning incense, tapers lighted at noonday, and a wafer god, would treat him as a fanatic, a heretick, a blasphemer; and, in my opinion, consistently enough with the rest of their conduct, who are so absurd and cruel as to mutilate young lads, in order to render their voices and praises more acceptable to an Almighty Being?

The country round *Turin* is nearly as pleasant as that of *Florence*; and, if you consider the beauty of the river, fully so: The city itself is, certainly, much more regular and handsome than any other in *Italy*, and would be a delightful abode, were a man well recommended and introduced into the best company; for our notions and characters of places often depend on the little accident of falling into agreeable or disagreeable society. The young *Englishmen* here, complain of the dulness and melancholy of the court, which throws a gloom over the whole face of *Turin*, as there is neither an *English* or a *French* ambassador here, the common resources of amusement and politeness, in the principal courts of *Europe*. The King, as I have intimated, prays much; the Duke of *Savoy* not a little; the Ladies in waiting are ancient, the same that adorned the drawing-room some thirty or forty years ago; then the Duke is the father of nine children, a circumstance which naturally renders a man somewhat serious in every station of life. All these things considered, you will imagine *Turin* is not so gay as it might have been under other circumstances. The women, however, are extremely beautiful and fair in this country, though, indeed, the Ladies of *Milan* and *Venice* almost vie with them in complexion and features. They have not yet, in any part of *Italy*, openly adopted the *French* mode of destroying the beauty which Nature has endowed them with, by laying red on their cheeks; and I believe there are fewer women here than in *England*, who have fallen into that unpleasing fashion. The degree to which this fairness of skin prevails in the northern

parts

LETTER LI.

parts of *Italy* is a little astonishing. I can hearken to a reasoner, who informs me, that the frequent mixture of the *Moors*, and their intermarriages with the *Spaniards*, during the several centuries they occupied so large a portion of *Spain*, will account for the olive complexion of that nation; but we are still at a loss to comprehend why the *French* are a browner people than the inhabitants of *Piedmont* and *Lombardy*, who live in nearly the same latitude. The common people are more olive-coloured than the gentry here, but that, perhaps, is owing to the heat of the sun; so that, in fact, they are rather sun-burnt than of a natural olive-colour. The women are so much handsomer than those in *Naples*, that on the first thought, one wonders that a *Neapolitan* of a large fortune, does not, for the sake of a fair offspring, seek a wife in these parts; but when it is considered how little the charms of beauty, affection, society, and constancy, are required in marriage here, the wonder ceases: Family connections, fortune, and an eldest son, seem to be the only objects of matrimony.

I go every night to the comedy. The company of comedians are from *Venice*, and
per-

perhaps are the best company in *Italy*; but, as I have mentioned in former letters, the drama all over *Italy* is in a very low state, and how a reformation should be effected I can hardly conceive. Their plays are generally dull, where they are not farcical; and where they are farcical, they descend to the ribaldry of our jack-puddings at *Bartholomew Fair*. How, therefore, should they ever have good actors, till their actors are furnished with better compositions, and better heard; and, what is also of equal consequence, better paid than at present? I must not, now I am upon the subject of plays, any longer forget to tell you, that at *Florence*, women, as with us, sit in the pit; a custom, I believe, peculiar to that city.

In the great guard-room, adjoining to the King's apartments, I see the same cobwebs I left there last year, and which, possibly, have subsisted ever since the beginning of this century. Strange, that in so elegant a palace there should be so glaring, so nasty a deformity; but it is in *England* only that a uniformity of grandeur and cleanliness bespeaks the riches of the master! In *Italy* you see some palaces with pictures and statues to the value of ten or twenty thousand pounds, and a bricked

floor

LETTER LI.

floor you would be ashamed of in your kitchen; then the hangings, chairs, and curtains, are such as an *English* Nobleman would blush to put into his garrets. Another instance, a striking one indeed, of parsimony mixed with royalty, is, that at this moment, both in the gardens at *Parma* and *Turin*, they are actually making hay in the small plots or partitions; and I should suppose, the quantity is rather an object of shillings than guineas; for the abundance of meadow grounds all through *Piedmont* and *Lombardy*, is really surprising.

I take pleasure in surveying the fortifications of *Turin*. I consider this state as our natural ally, from the nature of its situation; and it gives me the utmost delight to see the exact order in which they are kept: It appears to me, that if a brick decay, it is immediately supplied with a new one. The repairs of so many fortified towns in so small a principality, must fall heavily on the King's revenue; but there is an œconomy here practised in government an *Englishman* has no idea of: I have it from the best authority, that the appointments of the Secretary of State are about four hundred pounds a year sterling.

I am, Sir, &c.

LETTER LII.

Turin, *May* 1766.

SIR,

I THINK I have mentioned to you, how frequently I have blushed in *England* at the brutal custom which prevails amongst the common people there, of boxing upon every little quarrel; and how often I have since blushed in *Italy*, that I should have been ashamed of my country for a practice which I now esteem laudable, taking mankind such as they are. I find, by my experience here, that the sudden indignation and transports of a choleric man, must be immediately gratified, and when a bloody nose given on the spot, or the gentle and cooler method of challenging the offender to strip, does not satisfy, assassination will take place, and stabbing will be the substitute of boxing. I am led into the repetition of this remark by a story I picked up the other day in this city, which pleases me extremely, as it characterises so strongly the different geniuses of the *Italian* and the *English* common people. It seems that a few weeks since, some *English* sailors in the port of

of *Nice* had got drunk at a publick house, grew noisy and quarrelsome, stript into buff, and fought it out ; but the poor landlady, who expected nothing less from the outset of the fray than blood and murder, had, in the very beginning of it, run for the guard of the town, to take them into custody : The guard came as soon as possible ; but, before this period, the sailors had finished their battle, and, according to the *English* custom, had sat down to drink again, the best friends in the world, which they explained to the soldiers; but the soldiers not having the least comprehension of such sudden forgiveness and friendship, insisted that they should all go to the guardhouse : This obstinacy affronted our tars, who fell violently upon them, and, I think, broke two or three of their muskets ; but in the end they were overpowered, and one of them taken prisoner, the rest escaping to their ship. The sequel of the story is, that the commandant put the prisoner into the stocks all night, which is an infamous kind of punishment here, for they do not sit, but lie, (perhaps in the mud) on their backs: Now the prisoner happening to be the boatswain of the ship, he thought his dignity affronted

fronted, and lodged a complaint againſt the commandant, with the *Engliſh Chargé d' Affaires*, who reported it to the King. His Majeſty was very gracious, condemned the precipitancy of the commandant, who, he ſaid, ſhould have ſent to court for his inſtructions, laughed at the ridiculouſneſs of the event, but told the *Chargé d' Affaires*, that no reparation could be made, in any kingdom of the world, to a man, who had oppoſed the officers of juſtice, in the regular execution of their duty.

The frequency of ſtabbing in theſe countries, is not, however, merely owing to the ungovernableneſs of the paſſions; for, were men under more reſtraint, the crime, I am perſuaded, would be leſs common; but, here, beſides the ſanctuary which delinquents find in churches and holy places, there is another ſtill more open ſanctuary, I mean, the remiſſneſs both of law and proſecution. Mr *Murray*, our late reſident at *Venice*, upon his firſt arrival there, loudly proclaimed, that ſhould any *Engliſhman* be aſſaſſinated during his reſidentſhip, no expence, no interpoſition, ſhould prevent his bringing the criminal to condign puniſhment: The *Venetian* common people

people are all apprifed of his refolution, and that no *Englifhmen* has been murdered, he afcribes to this meafure. Sir *James Gray*, our late Envoy at *Naples*, I am told, was once extremely active in bringing a criminal to the gallows, who had affaffinated one of our countrymen. The example, perhaps, had a good effect on their behaviour, as there has been no fuch other inftance in all *Italy* fince that time; but it had little influence on their morals; for, the day happening to be black and ftormy, the common people believed that Heaven was offended at the execution of a Catholick for the death of a Heretick; fo far were they from imagining it was a proper juftice, and a facrifice pleafing to God. Could the church be prevailed on to recede from the right of fheltering murderers, it would be a great ftride towards a reformation of this enormous evil. At *Florence*, where Sir *Horatio Man* informed me that fewer capital crimes are committed than in any other city of *Italy*, my eyes were tired with the view of an affaffin and another delinquent, who had taken refuge on the fteps before a church contiguous to Lord ———'s houfe. We could not look out of window, but thefe fellows prefented sented themselves to our sight; they sauntered upon the steps all day, and retired into the church during the night. His Lordship told me they had led this life many months, and so badly do good people often judge of real charity, that it was esteemed a matter of religion in the neighbourhood to supply these wretches every day with a sufficiency of provision. I must not omit, however, to mention, that government, upon very extraordinary occasions, will sometimes encroach a little upon the privileges of the church. Not long ago, there was a murder, of a very atrocious nature, committed in that city, and the perpetrator, as usual, flew to a church for his asylum; upon which, the magistracy caused it to be surrounded night and day, with a guard sufficient to prevent any one from going to Mass there, and consequently from carrying him any sustenance. In a few days, the criminal, from a certainty of present death, by starving, threw himself into the hands of justice, to take his trial, when he met with his deserts.

I am, Sir, &c.

LETTER LIII.

Lyons, *May* 29, 1766.

SIR,

WE are this moment arrived at *Lyons*, without having suffered the least alarm from the passage of the *Alps*, which appeared so terrifying to some of us the last year. Certainly there cannot be produced a stronger instance of the power of use and practice, than the total banishment of fear, which we experienced upon this occasion; and, though I am well apprised that carpenters and bricklayers, from habit, work with the same indifference on the ridge of a house, that they do on the ground, I cannot but wonder at the composure with which we travelled so many miles, on the edges of so many precipices, having often on one hand, monstrous impending rocks, threatening to fall on our heads every moment; and, on the other, a boisterous torrent, some hundreds of feet below us, filled with vast fragments of those same rocks, which, from time to time, in the course of ages, have broken off and fallen into it.

Mount *Cenis* was in the worſt ſtate it ever can be; for we travelled over it not only in the worſt ſeaſon of the year, but alſo after as ſevere a winter as can be recollected in the memory of man; ſo that it was loaded with much greater quantities of ſnow than is uſual. The paſſage into *Italy* is compoſed of a very ſteep aſcent, almoſt three miles high; then of a plain, nearly flat, about five or ſix miles long; and, laſtly, of a deſcent, about ſix miles in length; ſo that you will conclude, the deſcent on the *Italian* ſide is not ſo ſteep as that on the ſide of *Savoy*. Each ſlope of the mountain is covered with large ſtones, ſome fixed in the ground, the others looſe: The plain is ſmooth, and full of good graſs. Both going and returning, when you arrive at the foot of the hill, your coach, or chaiſe, is taken to pieces, and carried upon mules to the other ſide, and you yourſelf are tranſported by two men, on a common ſtraw elbow chair, without any feet to it, fixed upon two poles, like a ſedan chair, with, a ſwinging foot-board to prop up your feet; but, though it be the work of two men only to carry you, ſix, and ſometimes eight, attend, in order to relieve one another. The whole way that
you

LETTER LIII.

you ride in this manner being fourteen or fifteen miles, when the perſon carried is corpulent, it is neceſſary to employ ten porters. Though I have deſcribed the riſe of both the hills to be extremely craggy, yet the chairmen, from long uſe, become ſo habituated to the footing, that, like goats, they ſeldom make a falſe ſtep, and you hardly advance fifty yards, before you are perſuaded, that there is very little danger in this method of tranſporting you. The plain upon the ſummit is almoſt even, ſo that, upon the whole, it is rather an amuſing, than a frightful paſſage in the ſummer. In the winter, excepting the cold (which it is eaſy to provide againſt,) the paſſage is ſtill more pleaſant; for the whole ſurface of the ground being covered with ſnow, to a conſiderable depth, the paths are hard and ſmooth, ſo that gentlemen, for the moſt part, deſcend the ſteep hill on the ſide of *Savoy* in ſledges, which is ſaid to be an agreeable and ſafe kind of paſſage. The only inconvenience which can occur in the winter, is, that in ſome parts, on the plain of the mountain, ſudden guſts and ſtorms of wind blow down vaſt heaps of ſnow from the mountains that overlook the

plain

plain, which may overwhelm a paffenger; but this feldom happens, as they avoid to carry people in windy weather, and likewife pretend to know when it ought to be expected; however, in our way over the fummit, we faw feveral of thefe accumulations, the work of the laft winter.

The fummer months may be efteemed *June*, *July*, *Auguft*, *September*, perhaps *October*, and part of *November*; for it is accidental how foon the deep fnows fall. The winter months are *December*, *January*, *February*, *March*, and, moft probably, *April*; or, if the fnow begin to melt at that time, it freezes again in the night, and is hard long enough in the morning to admit of a fafe and pleafant paffage: This is likewife the cafe the firft week or two in *May*; but it was our ill fortune to pafs over it on the twenty-third, and, unluckily, on a dreadful, rainy morning, fo that it is almoft impoffible to give you a true idea of the badnefs of the road; neverthelefs, with all this difagreeablenefs, there was nothing to terrify us but the dangerous fituation of the poor chairmen; for, with regard to ourfelves, if they let us fall, which they did feveral times, we fell but the diftance of two

feet

feet, on foft fnow: I really think, therefore, that the only horror which attended it, was the danger of the poor men breaking their legs; for, the fnow being rotten and deceitful in feveral places, when they thought they had a good footing, they fometimes funk into it deeper than their knees, and fo let us drop gently on the ground. Another evil waiting on thefe deep fnows, are fprings, which leave a furface of fnow on their tops, and may aptly be compared to quickfands: One of thefe we faw in our paffage, with a dead horfe lying on the brink of it: It feems that a boy had, the day before, not being apprized of the well, either rid or driven the horfe into it, and was unable to extricate it by himfelf.

An axle-tree of my carriage breaking down amongft the *Alps*, I availed myfelf of the misfortune.—As I was near the place where the Chevalier *de Bellifle* was killed in his attempt to force a way into *Piedmont*, I hired a mule, and rode near the fpot to take a view of the field of battle; it is a fmall diftance from the high road, contiguous to which is a fortification, called *La Brunetta*, which, with more reafon than is ufual, may be ftyled impregnable. It was built foon after the

peace

peace of *Utrecht*, and being formed out of the solid rock, which faces the road to *Susa*, renders the passage of an army that way impracticable now, which was formerly very easy. *Belleisle* was so fixed in the opinion of the impregnableness of *La Brunetta,* that he chose rather to attack the pass of the intrenchments on the heights of *Exilles* into *Piedmont*, a method supposed by many, at that time, and by all now, still more desperate. Every body remembers that signal defeat, where, from the advantage of situation, a few *Piedmontese* easily vanquished a numerous gallant *French* army.

Nature seems to have formed a barrier betwixt *France* and *Italy* ; and the present King of *Sardinia* is very assiduous in strengthening it by art, all the fortifications being not only kept in excellent repair, but daily improved and augmented. You remember how the *French* were baffled at *Coni*, though they had taken *Demont,* beaten the army which came to its relief, and carried on the siege to all appearance with the utmost success; yet, as it was undertaken late in the season, the snows fell before they had finished their operations, and rendered all they had done of no effect.

Never-

Nevertheless, the wonderful strength of *La Brunetta*, will, probably, compel the *French*, if ever they shall again invade *Piedmont*, to enter by *Coni*, as the more eligible alternative, where both are so hazardous. It is true, there are some other openings into *Piedmont*, but they are esteemed by the military men still more impracticable.

I met with an old Monk in *Savoy*, whose knowledge of men, and the world, astonished me, till I learnt he had passed the younger years of his life in armies. He informed me that hay, in the *French* camp, in 1747, sold for six-pence *English* a pound, which circumstance alone was almost sufficient to ruin an expedition. It was all brought from *France* on mules, and each mule consumed a great part of his load, which was the cause of its excessive dearness. He told me, that the commander of the *French* army, after the war in 1736, returning home from *Italy*, through the town *(La Chambre)* where he resides, said, " Father, by my master's alli-
" ance with the King of *Sardinia*, we have
" now leave to march peaceably into *France*;
" but, for these two hundred years past, (and
" I believe it will always be the same thing)
" the

" the *French* have constantly been kicked
" home; (*coups de pied au ventre*, was the ex-
" pression.")

We are so accustomed to consider the inhabitants of *Savoy* as Mountaineers, and a savage race of men, that I was extremely surprised to find them docile, not to say polished; but now, that I am better acquainted with the state of the country, I no longer wonder that their behaviour is such as a frequent commerce with strangers will naturally produce. I have intimated before, that the winter is no impediment to travelling in this part of the world; for the snow renders the whole road excellent, and, in some of the rough craggy ways, much better than in the summer; so that there are people continually passing into *Italy* through the *Alps*. At one of the inns, I asked the servant maid if they were not often a long time without seeing company? " Yes, said she, sometimes,
" in the winter, we are three or four days
" without seeing a soul, and then they come
" in such crouds, that we can hardly provide
" beds for them." From this answer, you may gather how much this road is frequented; nor would I have you suppose the accommodation is such as I described in the
road

LETTER LIII.

road from *Loretto* to *Rome*, or from *Rome* to *Naples*; far from it; some of the cooks are good, and also some of the provisions. I will not boast of the bed-chambers, but they are excellent in comparison of those in the above-mentioned roads. Certainly *Savoy* is a dismal barren district, in competition with the generality of the kingdoms in the southern parts of *Europe*; yet there are many fertile spots in it, and, during the first and second day's journey from *Lyons*, one would almost be tempted to call a considerable extent of it, a plentiful country. I had heard, the six provinces brought in a very trifling revenue to the King, but my old Monk assured me, that the taxes of all kinds amounted to considerably above one hundred thousand pounds sterling a year. When you approach towards the very barren parts, every one of the peasants is in possession of a small quantity of ground, which he cultivates for the maintainance of his family; and there is hardly an instance of a man's labouring by the day in these parts. It is supposed that there are generally sixty thousand *Savoyards* absent from home, during the winter; for those who have no vineyards, as soon as they have gotten in

their

their little harveſt, and ſown their ſeed, ſet out, ſome for *France*, ſome for *Italy*, and others for different parts, in order to procure a ſmall pittance, which they bring home to their wives and children. When I paſſed, ſoon after harveſt, the laſt year, thro' *Savoy*, I was amazed at the prodigious number of ſmall ſtacks of corn ſpread over the face of the country; in ſome places like hay-cocks in a meadow; but this partition of the country, into ſuch an infinity of ſmall farms, accounts for the appearance; beſides, that the peaſants make their ſtacks ſmall, from a perſuaſion, that, if they were larger, the corn in that climate would become diſcoloured and muſty. I aſked my friend, the Monk, if theſe poor people preſerved the ſame character of integrity in foreign kingdoms they did formerly; in anſwer to which, he told me a ſtory I had heard a thouſand times at *Paris*; " How the *Savoyards* in that city having detected one of their brethren in ſome piece of roguery, thought it ſuch a diſgrace to the whole body, that they determined to make an example of him; and, in conſequence, obliged him to run the gantlet, the whole length of the *Place Royale*. Their diſtribu-
-tion

tion of juſtice gave ſome offence to government, but the King laugh'd it off, and ſo it ended."—I muſt not, however, omit mentioning, to the diſhonour of the *Savoyards*, that, in our way through the *Alps*, laſt year, on the evening of a feſtival, we met great numbers of them returning home from their merry meeting, and, I think, I never ſaw in *England* a ſtronger example of drunkenneſs; they ſeemed to be every one of them more or leſs jolly: Whether it were accident, or whether it were cuſtomary, I do not know, but it never happened to me, during my ſtay in *Italy*, to ſee ſuch a ſight.

I am, Sir, &c.

LETTER LIV.

Lyons, *June* 1766.

SIR,

WHEN I paſſed the *Alps* into *Italy*, laſt year, I made ſome ſhort memorandums of what I obſerved amongſt thoſe mountains. I propoſe now, by the help of theſe notes, to give you a few miſcellaneous remarks on that country, which will finiſh my accounts of *Italy*.

A man advances but a little way into the mountainous country, before he perceives many of the natives, of both sexes, labouring under that species of swelled throat, which the common people call the *Deer's Neck*, and the medical people a *Bronchocele*. I was apprised, before I went into *Savoy*, that in what place soever the inhabitants drink snow water, they are subject to this distemper; but I had not the least idea of such an universality; for, as you approach towards Mount Cenis, you find very few exempt from it; and many of those swellings are so enormous, and of so loathsome an appearance, especially in ugly, ragged, half starved old women, that the very sight of them turns the stomach. I do not learn, upon enquiry, that the malady is ever mortal; not but that sometimes the tumour compresses the wind-pipe so much, as to render respiration very difficult, which, at the long run, though insensibly, may affect life. I was curious in my examination, whether any children were born with this malady upon them: I did not know but that the blood of the mother, imbued with snow-water, might operate this effect upon the fœtus before the birth; however, I was informed,

formed, to my satisfaction, that there is no such instance, and even that the swelling never begins to form, till towards two years of age, some examples of which I myself saw.

The river *Arc* accompanies the road two days journey of the seven, and affords much speculation and entertainment to the traveller, who has no concern upon him; but the horrid quantity of vast fragments fallen into it from the impending rocks, and the noisy foaming of the waters against those fragments, add to the terror of such who are already frightened at the precipices. In most places the rivers swell in winter; but amongst cold mountains they are almost empty in that season; for, there, what generally falls, is snow, which lodges all the winter; or, if it rain, the rain is soon converted into ice, which lodges also; so that it is in the summer months, and chiefly in *July*, when the snows and ice are melting, that this river is fullest. Where it happens to be narrow, and where, by accident, there is a considerable collection of fragments, the stream dashes with such rapidity against them, as to resemble not only the sound, but, in some degree, the very appearance of cascades. From the heights of the mountains you see, in various parts, a little torrent of melted snow, making its way down into the bed of the river with great velocity: Some of these torrents are small channels; others, by length of time, have carried away the soil, and acquired the breadth of one or two, and even three feet. The industry of the *Savoyard* has availed him of these currents of water; for there are very few of them which are not directed to some use. The frequent accidents which happened to my carriage amongst those mountains, brought me much acquainted with the blacksmiths there, and I was exceedingly pleased to find in several of their shops, not only their bellows blown, and their grindstones turned, but also a monstrous heavy hammer for forging iron, worked by these streams. I do not, however, speak of this mechanism as a new thing; I know, that in our iron and copper-mills, it is carried to the highest perfection; but I mean to tell you that the *Savoyard* is not in such a state of barbarism as you may possibly suspect.

There is so much rocky and barren ground in *Savoy*, particularly towards Mount *Cenis*, that the least spot of earth capable of producing

cing corn or grafs, does not lie uncultivated, and you see all through the country, one or the other growing on the slope of the rocks, wherever the peasant can find a little piece of flat surface, with a depth of soil sufficient to admit of vegetation. Many of these pieces of land are not bigger, and many are less than the hall of an old *English* country mansion-house; but, in some places, they are numerous, and, by hanging one over the other, from the top to the bottom of the hill, make a pleasant picture. I have more than once, upon this journey, had occasion to speak of the providential and blind partiality which almost every individual feels for his native country. I do not know that I ever met with so great and so enviable a degree of it in any man, as in my good friend the Monk I spoke of in my last letter. Whilst I was conversing with him, I turned my eyes towards two or three of these little patches of cultivated ground, encompassed with a monstrous extent of barren rock, and, feeling some compassion for the supposed misery of the inhabitants, I opened my mouth to say something on that subject; but he imagining that I meant a panegyric on the state of their agriculture,

culture, interrupted me, with great eagerness, saying, *Aye, God be praised, we are not like other nations, dependent for our food upon a due course of the seasons; for whether the rains or the droughts prevail, we are always assured of our harvest; we have so many crops on the bottom, the middle, and the summits of the mountains, that, when some fail, the others necessarily succeed.*—You may imagine I did not awaken him out of his pleasing dream, and, indeed, I must have been a brute had I attempted to open his eyes.

When I first entered into *Savoy*, I saw but very little snow on the tops of the hills; but, as I advanced towards higher hills, I could not but admire at the quantities which still remained unmelted at the end of *August*; though there was none but what lay on that side of the mountains which faced the North, the North-East, and East; a proof, however, of what little efficacy are the early and oblique rays of the sun on great heights. But why do I wonder at so familiar a phænomenon? All the world is informed, that very high mountains are covered with eternal snows, and that even the meridian rays of the sun are impotent, at a certain elevation

from

LETTER LIV.

from the earth; of which I afterwards saw examples in abundance.

Mount *Cenis* is, certainly, a very high mountain, but it is the road, and not its superior height, which has rendered it so celebrated. When you arrive at the plain I have before described (on its top) there are, both on your right, and on your left, still higher mountains; and, as you descend towards *Piedmont*, you see, on your left hand, *Notre Dame de la Neige*, which is reputed by some to be the highest mountain in *Europe* on the Continent: it is always covered with snow; and, generally, to such a depth as renders the road impassable; but, when the year is favourable, the inhabitants of the neighbouring districts make a kind of pilgrimage to the chapel. It is computed, that, in 1764, three thousand peasants laboured up the hill, to hear Mass there. Churches, chapels, and convents, on the summits of mountains, are common through all *Italy*: The *Italians*, like the idolaters of old times, chuse to worship and burn incense on their high places.

I am, Sir, &c.

An Admonition to Gentlemen who pass the Alps, *and make the Tour of* Italy.

AT *Lyons*, or *Geneva*, the Voiturins, (men who furnish horses for the journey over the *Alps*,) make their demands according to the number of travellers who are on the spot, or (as they hear) are on the road. If there be but few, they are sometimes very reasonable; if there be many, they rise in their demands, and even confederate not to take less than a certain exorbitant sum, stipulated amongst themselves. When there are but few travellers going on, he who takes a passenger has a very good chance upon his arrival at *Turin*, to find customers back again, and, therefore, will agree on very moderate terms. The price of a voiturin and pair of horses is, generally, from eight to ten or eleven louis (guineas,) besides the present of a louis, or at least half a louis, at the end of the journey; however, without accidents to enhance the price, one may expect a pair of horses for eight or nine louis.

Some

Some travellers have not a chaise of their own, but pass the *Alps* in the voiturin's chaise, in which case, the voiturin will sometimes take a man still a louis cheaper, because, when he arrives at *Turin*, he, by this means, has a double chance of bringing back a traveller; for, if the traveller have no chaise himself, the voiturin has one ready for him; and, if he have a chaise, the voiturin leaves his at *Turin* till an opportunity offer of returning it.

In going from *Geneva* to *Turin*, I paid thirty-one louis for six horses and three voiturins; *viz.* four horses for my coach, and two for my chaise; but then both the coach and the chaise were very heavy. On my return to *Turin*, a voiturin offered to bring me to *Lyons*, the day after my arrival, for twenty-eight louis, but as I chose to make some stay there, this voiturin went off with other Gentlemen, and several travellers happening to come in, none of the voiturins would take me unless I hired six horses to the coach, and paid thirty-six louis, which I was obliged to submit to; and, had I deferred it one day longer, I must have paid forty, as I afterwards learnt from one who set out the following day with the same equipage as mine. It seems the voiturins prefer chaises to coaches, as they demand usually in a higher proportion for a coach and four, than for a chaise and two.

    The voiturins, for this sum, defray your charges on the road; they pay for your dinner, supper, and lodging; so that the seven days journey from *Geneva* or *Lyons*, to *Turin*, costs little more than what you contract for with them, the extraordinaries being only the small presents made to the servants, and the expence of breakfasting. The voiturins are generally obliging and busy in providing the best eatables the country affords, because they pay the same ordinary, whether the innkeepers give you good or bad provisions; besides, they are all ambitious of character, which procures them recommendations from one traveller to another. The voiturin is likewise at the whole expence of carrying you and your equipage over Mount *Cenis*, except a little gratuity which every Gentleman gives to the poor chairmen, perhaps sixpence to each, and a little drink at the resting place, or half way house. As the voiturins are obliged to hire a number of mules, in proportion to the quantity of luggage, and the weight of the chaise, or coach, this consideration

ration, besides the draught for their horses, makes them raise their demands when the equipage is heavy. I would advise no Gentleman to hire horses by the day, and pay for his diet, lodging, and passage over Mount *Cenis*, as he will be much imposed on in many of these articles; but, if he be so inclined, the voiturins will furnish horses at four *Savoy* livres a day each, allowing seven days for going, and seven days for returning, that is, for a chaise and a pair, fourteen times eight livres, about five pounds eighteen shillings; but this, as I have intimated, turns out a dearer method of travelling, and is never to be practised.

The trouble and expence of taking a carriage to pieces, and transporting it over the mountain, lying entirely on the voiturin, except a small present to the coach-maker, it is only to satisfy curiosity that I here give the particular rates, charged by an ordinance of his *Sardinian* Majesty, to prevent disputes and impositions.

Every person who is carried over Mount *Cenis* in a chair, is obliged to employ six chairmen, or, if he be lusty, eight; or extremely corpulent, ten; of which, and, indeed, of all disputable matters, the Syndics are ap-

appointed by his Majesty absolute judges. The Syndics are magistrates, living the one at *Lanneburg*, on this side of the mountain, and the other at *Novaleze*, which is situated at the other foot of the mountain, on the side towards *Turin*; they are poor men, and not above accepting a small present for drink, but are invested with sufficient power to compel both the muleteers and the chairmen to attend, when any traveller arrives. I had an opportunity, when I went into *Italy*, of seeing this power exerted; for the chairmen were in the midst of their harvest, gathering in the produce of their own little farms, and would gladly have been excused. The Syndic, therefore, rung the alarum-bell, which summons was immediately obeyed, and a sufficient number of them were selected to transport me and my company the next morning.

The pay to each chairman is fifty sous of *Savoy*, that is, two shillings and seven-pence halfpenny. The pay for a mule to carry over a servant is forty sous, about two shillings and a penny. The pay for each mule which carries the baggage is fifty sous, two shillings and seven pence halfpenny.

A mule

A mule is not obliged, by the ordinance, to carry above three hundred and fifty pounds; therefore, if the body of the coach, or chaise, or any parcel of luggage weigh more, it is in the breast of the muleteers to demand what sum they please; a privilege they seldom neglect to avail themselves of, and, sometimes, with great extortion, to the amount of many guineas; therefore, above all men, the *English*, who are reputed rich, should contract with the voiturins to defray this expence. Some *Italians*, who pass often over the mountains, build the body of their coach as light as possible, and of such a structure that it may be separated into two parts, by which contrivance they transport it on the cheapest terms. *Englishmen*, who take their own coaches, should provide such a carriage as may be taken to pieces, which those with a perch do not admit of.

A man may travel post, if he pleases, through the *Alps*, but it is attended with some trouble; and, as I would not advise any one to drive fast on the edges of those precipices, I shall forbear to enter into any detail on that subject.

When you arrive in *Piedmont*, you travel either by the *Poſt*, or the *Cambiatura*. A foreigner is ſurpriſed at the diſtinction, when he finds there is no difference betwixt the two, except the price; the payment for the poſt being conſiderably higher than for the Cambiatura; but the poſt-horſes are the ſame, and the ſpeed in travelling is the ſame. It may therefore be concluded, that every body chuſes the Cambiatura. I ſhould, however, to be minute, mention that there is one difference, though I have ſaid there is none; for if a man travel in the night, he is obliged to pay the price of the poſt. I believe I do not exactly know the hiſtory of the Cambiatura, but whatever was originally the deſign, and the practice, every man now eaſily procures an order for it. The ſame thing happens with regard to the *Bolletino* in the ſtate of *Venice*, which anſwers to the Cambiatura in *Lombardy*. Both the Cambiatura and the Bolletino, are orders to the poſt-maſters to furniſh horſes at the low price; but I was never called upon to ſhew them at any of the poſt-houſes.

Through all *Italy*, the poſts are, upon an average,

average, eight or nine miles, and, perhaps, in *Piedmont*, a little more.

In the *Venetian* state, if a man travel by the post, he must pay sixteen livres and a half for his horses, three livres to the postilion, and half a livre to the hostler, making in all twenty livres, about ten shillings; but as no gentleman travels without a Bolletino, the expence is, eleven livres for the horses, three to the postilions, and half a livre to the hostler, in all about seven shillings and three-pence per post.

In the Ecclesiastical State, there is no distinction betwixt the Post and the Cambiatura; and the Post is cheaper than in the other states of *Italy*. Every post there, is but eight pauls and a half, three pauls to the postilion, and half a paul to the hostler. A paul is about six-pence. It may be remarked, that the *Italian* Princes give only two pauls to the postilions; but, so much is expected from *Englishmen*, that, to avoid trouble, and even insults, it is adviseable to pay them three pauls. I knew a nobleman, who, from his princely disposition, gave the postilions five shillings a post, though even that sum did not content them; but such instances of generosity nerofity render it very difagreeable to future *Englifh* travellers, who are all fuppofed to be Lords, and are expected by the poftilions to follow the moft extravagant examples. No *Englifhman* fhould, therefore, pay more than three pauls, which is a greater reward than a poftilion in *England* receives, where other wages are higher, and the neceffaries of life dearer than in *Italy*.

Through *Piedmont* and the *Milanefe*, poft-horfes are dearer than in the other parts of *Italy*, the payment, together with the eighteen pence given to the poftilion, and fomething to the hoftler, amounting to about ten fhillings per poft.

From *Rome* to *Naples* you may travel poft, but the road is fo bad, in fome places, that I would rather advife the moderate rate of travelling with a voiturin. The moft eligible method is, to leave your own carriage at *Rome*, and to go in the chaife belonging to the voiturin; he will carry you (I always fuppofe two perfons) for about four pounds fterling, and pay for your fupper and lodging; however, the accommodation is fo wretched on the *Neapolitan* road, that every gentleman fhould furnifh himfelf with fuch cold provifion

sion and wine, as will subsist him four or five days.

I would not advise any gentleman to travel with voiturins in the other parts of *Italy*, unless it be necessary for the state of his finances, to take the cheapest method. In point of œconomy it certainly is preferable; but it is extremely tedious, as they seldom go above two miles and three quarters in an hour, and what is equally uncomfortable, carry you to the dirtiest and most noisome inns on the road.

F I N I S.

www.ingramcontent.com/pod-product-compliance
Lightning Source LLC
Chambersburg PA
CBHW030803230426
43667CB00008B/1041